WILLIAMS

in an hour

BY MICHAEL PALLER

SUSAN C. MOORE, SERIES EDITOR

PLAYWRIGHTS in an hour
know the playwright, love the play

IN AN HOUR BOOKS • HANOVER, NEW HAMPSHIRE • INANHOURBOOKS.COM
AN IMPRINT OF SMITH AND KRAUS PUBLISHERS, INC • SMITHANDKRAUS.COM

With grateful thanks to Carl R. Mueller, whose fascinating introductions to his translations of the Greek and German playwrights provided inspiration for this series.

Published by In an Hour Books
an imprint of Smith and Kraus, Inc.
177 Lyme Road, Hanover, NH 03755
inanhourbooks.com SmithandKraus.com

Know the playwright, love the play.

In an Hour, In a Minute, and Theater IQ are registered trademarks of In an Hour Books.

© 2009 by In an Hour Books, an imprint of Smith and Kraus Publishers, Inc.
All rights reserved
Manufactured in the United States of America
First Edition: April 2010
10 9 8 7 6 5 4 3 2 1

All rights reserved including the right of reproduction in whole or in
part in any form except for use in reviews of the book and/or series.
Please direct inquiries to In an Hour Books (603) 643-6431.

CAMINO REAL. © 1953 by The University of the South. Copyright renewed. Reprinted by permission of New Directions Publishing Corp. For performance rights, contact Dramatists Play Service, 440 Park Ave. S, New York, NY 10016 (www.dramatists.com) (212-683-8960).

CAT ON A HOT TIN ROOF. © 1954 by The University of the South. Copyright renewed. Reprinted by permission of New Directions Publishing Corp. For performance rights, contact Dramatists Play Service, 440 Park Ave. S, New York, NY 10016 (www.dramatists.com) (212-683-8960).

THE GLASS MENAGERIE. © 1945 by The University of the South AND Edwin D. Williams. Copyright renewed. Reprinted by permission of New Directions Publishing Corp. For performance rights, contact Dramatists Play Service, 440 Park Ave. S, New York, NY 10016 (www.dramatists.com) (212-683-8960).

A STREETCAR NAMED DESIRE. © 1947 by The University of the South. Copyright renewed. Reprinted by permission of New Directions Publishing Corp. For performance rights, contact Dramatists Play Service, 440 Park Ave. S, New York, NY 10016 (www.dramatists.com) (212-683-8960).

VIEUX CARRE. © 1977 by The University of the South. Copyright renewed. Reprinted by permission of New Directions Publishing Corp. For performance rights, contact Dramatists Play Service, 440 Park Ave. S, New York, NY 10016 (www.dramatists.com) (212-683-8960).

Front cover design by Dan Mehling, dmehling@gmail.com
Text design by Kate Mueller, Electric Dragon Productions
Book production by Dede Cummings Design, DCDesign@sover.net

ISBN-13: 978-1-936232-32-1
ISBN-10: 1-936232-32-4
Library of Congress Control Number: 2009943224

CONTENTS

Why Playwrights in an Hour?

This new series by Smith and Kraus Publishers titled Playwrights in an Hour has a dual purpose for being: one academic, the other general. For the general reader, this volume, as well as the many others in the series, offers in compact form the information needed for a basic understanding and appreciation of the works of each volume's featured playwright. Which is not to say that there don't exist volumes on end devoted to each playwright under consideration. But inasmuch as few are blessed with enough time to read the splendid scholarship that is available, a brief, highly focused accounting of the playwright's life and work is in order. The central feature of the series, a thirty- to forty-page essay, integrates the playwright into the context of his or her time and place. The volumes, though written to high standards of academic integrity, are accessible in style and approach to the general reader as well as to the student and, of course, to the theater professional and theatergoer. These books will serve for the brushing up of one's knowledge of a playwright's career, to the benefit of theater work or theatergoing. The Playwrights in an Hour series represents all periods of Western theater: Aeschylus to Shakespeare to Wedekind to Ibsen to Williams to Beckett, and on to the great contemporary playwrights who continue to offer joy and enlightenment to a grateful world.

Carl R. Mueller
School of Theater, Film and Television
Department of Theater
University of California, Los Angeles

Introduction

Tennessee Williams was the first American playwright to bring a lyric sensibility to the stage. Eugene O'Neill had the makings of a poet, but as T. S. Eliot once remarked about George Bernard Shaw, "the poet in him was still-born," and most of his characters are stammerers. Arthur Miller occasionally achieved a powerful urban music, particularly in *Death of a Salesman*, but the structure of that play was probably inspired by Williams' *Glass Menagerie*.

Williams had a remarkable ear for the florid vocabulary of the South. Because he was also influenced by such troubadours as Hart Crane and Garcia Lorca and D.H. Lawrence, he had a natural affinity for metaphor and a way with form that was penetrating and unique. The tension between a sensitive nature in a harsh environment was his great underlying theme: a conflict between what is delicate and poetic in American life and that which is unfeeling, brutalizing, and coarse. This, of course, is the basic conflict of *A Streetcar Named Desire* as reflected in the opposition between Blanche DuBois, an aristocratic Southern belle, and Stanley Kowalski, a crude Polish auto mechanic. But in Williams, this opposition is never simplistic. He knows there is decadence and corruption in the delicate Blanche, just as there is energy and life in the insensitive Stanley. Like Anton Chekhov, Williams both loves cherry orchards, but knows that there is more to them than their beauty. That is why he celebrates his fallen heroines — Laura in *The Glass Menagerie*, Alma in *Summer and Smoke*, Catherine in *Suddenly Last Summer* — while recognizing how they contribute to their own destruction.

That destruction often comes by way of castration, whether physical or mental. Williams created a large number of women and men who are either lobotomized or rendered impotent by the harsh paternalist values of the Southern Gothic culture. Chance Wayne in *Sweet Bird of Youth;*

Brick in *Cat on a Hot Tin Roof;* Val Xavier in *Orpheus Descending* are instances of such characters. But he also created plenty of threatening males — Big Daddy in *Cat on a Hot Tin Roof,* Boss Finley in *Sweet Bird of Youth,* Jabe Torrance in *Orpheus Descending* — and occasional females. The often ruthless matrons — Amanda Wingfield in *The Glass Menagerie,* Lady Torrance in *Orpheus Descending,* Alexandra Del Lago in *Sweet Bird of Youth* — love their men so long as they can control and dominate them.

Blanche DuBois insists that she must have magic. The art of Tennessee Williams, which continues to be unparalleled, provides that magic without losing touch with reality.

Robert Brustein
Founding director of the Yale and American Repertory Theatres,
Distinguished Scholar in Residence, Suffolk University
Senior Research Fellow, Harvard University

Williams

IN A MINUTE

AGE	DATE	
—	1911	Enter Thomas Lanier Williams, March 26.
3	1914	Babe Ruth signs as a pitcher for the Boston Red Sox.
5	1916	Einstein proposes general theory of relativity.
8	1919	Prohibition begins in the United States.
9	1920	"The Flapper" hits the big screen, popularizing bobs, jazz, and short skirts.
11	1922	James Joyce — *Ulysses*
15	1926	Ernest Hemingway — *The Sun Also Rises*
18	1929	U.S. stock market crash
22	1933	*Esquire* debuts as the first men's magazine.
24	1935	German parliament legislates Nuremberg limiting the rights of Jewish citizens.
26	**1937**	**Tennessee Williams — *Candles to the Sun;* first full-length play premieres in St Louis in amateur production**
28	1939	*The Wizard of Oz*
30	1941	Japan launches surprise attack on Pearl Harbor.
33	**1944**	**Tennessee Williams — *The Glass Menagerie***
34	1945	Churchill, Stalin, and Roosevelt meet at Yalta to establish a new world order.
36	**1947**	**Tennessee Williams — *A Streetcar Named Desire***
37	1948	Alfred Kinsey — *Sexual Behavior in the Human Male*
41	1952	Rocky Marcino knocks out "Jersey Joe" Wolcott, wins heavy weight crown.
42	1953	Samuel Beckett — *Waiting for Godot*
44	**1955**	**Tennessee Williams — *Cat on a Hot Tin Roof***
45	1956	Prince Ranier of Monaco marries Grace Kelly.
46	1957	Fearing Soviet aggression, Western powers form NATO.
50	**1961**	**Tennessee Williams — *The Night of the Iguana***
52	1963	Beatle-mania sweeps the United Kingdom.
56	1967	Youth converge on San Francisco for a summer of love.
57	1968	Martin Luther King Jr. is assassinated at the Lorraine Motel in Memphis.
58	1969	Stonewall Riots in New York City energize the Gay Rights movement.
69	**1980**	**Tennessee Williams — *Will Mr. Merriwether Return from Memphis?***
71	1982	Wisconsin is the first state to outlaw discrimination based on sexual orientation.
72	**1983**	**Exit Tennessee Williams, February 25.**

A snapshot of the playwright's world. From historical events to pop-culture and the literary landscape of the time, this brief list catalogues events that directly or indirectly impacted the playwright's writing. Play citations refer to opening dates.

HIS WORKS

PLAYS

Candles to the Sun

The Fugitive Kind

Spring Storm, 1937–38, produced in 1999

Not About Nightingales, 1938, produced in 1998

Battle of Angels

The Last of My Solid Gold Watches, written about 1942, produced 1947

The Glass Menagerie

27 Wagons Full of Cotton, written about 1944, produced 1955

You Touched Me! (with Donald Windham)

The Unsatisfactory Supper, written about 1945, produced 1986

A Streetcar Named Desire

Summer and Smoke

The Rose Tattoo

Camino Real

Cat on a Hot Tin Roof

Orpheus Descending

Garden District, comprised of Something Unspoken and Suddenly Last
        Summer

Sweet Bird of Youth

Period of Adjustment

The Night of the Iguana

The Milk Train Doesn't Stop Here Anymore

Slapstick Tragedy, comprised of The Gnädiges Fräulein and The Mutilated

The Two-Character Play

Kingdom of Earth (The Seven Descents of Myrtle)

In the Bar of a Tokyo Hotel

This section presents a complete list of the playwright's works in chronological order by date written.

OTHER WORKS

Onstage with Williams:

Introducing Colleagues and Contemporaries
of Tennessee Williams

 THEATER

Anton Chekhov, Russian playwright

Federico García Lorca, Spanish poet and playwright

William Inge, American playwright

Eugene Ionesco, French playwright

Arthur Miller, American playwright

Eugene O'Neill, American playwright

Harold Pinter, English playwright

Wole Soyinka, Nigerian playwright and author

 ARTS

Marc Chagall, French painter

Aaron Copland, American composer

Salvador Dalí, Spanish artist

Georgia O'Keefe, American artist

Pablo Picasso, Spanish artist

Jackson Pollock, American painter

Mark Rothko, American painter

Igor Stravinsky, Russian composer

 FILM

Marlon Brando, American actor

Richard Burton, English actor

James Dean, American actor

Federico Fellini, Italian filmmaker

This section gives a list of contemporaries, whom the playwright may or may not have known. This can help you understand the intellectual, cultural, and historical times the playwright lived in. Eight contemporaries are shown in each category.

Katherine Hepburn, American actress
Vivien Leigh, English actress
François Truffaut, French filmmaker
Orson Welles, American filmmaker, actor

POLITICS/ MILITARY

Winston Churchill, English prime minister
Dwight Eisenhower, American president
Queen Elizabeth, English head of state
Adolf Hitler, German political leader
Saddam Hussein, Iraqi president
John F. Kennedy, American president
Joseph Stalin, Soviet leader
Malcolm X, American civil rights activist

SCIENCE

Lise Meitner, Austrian physicist
Enrico Fermi, Italian physicist
J. Robert Oppenheimer, American physicist
Dian Fossey, American zoologist
Fritz Strassmann, German chemist
Alexander Flemming, Scottish biologist and pharmacologist
Edwin Hubble, American astronomer
Jonas Salk, American virologist

LITERATURE

Italo Calvino, Italian writer
Truman Capote, American writer
Hart Crane, American poet
T. S. Eliot, American-English poet
William Faulkner, American novelist
D. H. Lawrence, English writer
Flannery O'Connor, American writer
Alexander Solzhenitsyn, Russian writer

RELIGION/ PHILOSOPHY

Simone de Beauvoir, French writer

Martin Luther King Jr., American minister, civil rights activist

Ayn Rand, American novelist

Jean-Paul Sartre, French philosopher

C. S. Lewis, Irish theologian and writer

Noam Chomsky, American philosopher

Dalai Lama, Tibetan religious and political leader

Mohandas Gandhi, Indian political and spiritual leader

SPORTS

Babe Ruth, American baseball player

Jackie Robinson, American baseball player

Jesse Owens, American track and field athlete

Helen Wills Moody, American tennis player

René Lacoste, French tennis player

Arnold Palmer, American golfer

Wilma Rudolf, American track and field athlete

Roger Bannister, English runner

INDUSTRY/ BUSINESS

Henry Ford, American industrialist

William Hearst, American newspaper magnate

William Fox, American founder of Fox Film Corporation

Rupert Murdoch, Australian media mogul

Adolph Zukor, Hungarian film mogul

Walt and Roy Disney, American founders of Disney

Sebastian Kresge, American founder of Kmart

Masaru Ibuka, Japanese cofounder of Sony

WILLIAMS

in an
hour

[NOTE ON QUOTATIONS: Tennessee Williams was very free and idiosyncratic in his use of ellipses. To distinguish his from mine, the latter appear in brackets.]

PRELIMINARIES

Tennessee Williams (1911–1983) was one of the leading figures in the American theater in the twentieth century. He created a lyrical, poetic expression never heard in the American theater before and, through his use of cinematic, nonrealistic settings, opened new opportunities for visual lyricism in American stage design. The roles he created for women were the greatest in the American theater in the years between 1944 and 1961. He was also a prolific writer of stories and poetry.

EARLY YEARS

Tennessee Williams was born Thomas Lanier Williams on March 26, 1911, in Columbus, Mississippi. His mother, Edwina Estelle Dakin, born in Ohio but raised in the South, affected the airs of a genteel

---

This is the core of the book. The essay places the playwright in the context of his or her world and analyzes the influences and inspirations within that world.

Southern belle all of her life. Her father was the Reverend Walter Edwin Dakin, an Episcopal minister whose interests, when not preaching or visiting parishioners, included reading widely from his large library that emphasized the classics, including Shakespeare. Her mother, Rosina Otte Dakin, was active in community events and devoted to music. Edwina grew up in this cultivated atmosphere, and while she didn't inherit these specific interests, she always conceived of herself as possessing an aura of generalized culture and civility — as befitted a member, and eventually a regent, of the Daughters of the American Revolution. She was a strict puritan when it came to sex, which she hated, and she tried to instill this attitude in her children, with disastrous results.

Williams' father, Cornelius Coffin Williams (known as C. C.), came from a distinguished line of pioneers who fought in the American Revolution and were prominent in the founding of Tennessee (two early American poets were also among his forebears, Tristram Coffin and Sidney Lanier). His mother died when he was five, and he was raised by his father and aunts. He was educated first in a seminary in Rogersville, Tennessee, and then in the Bell Buckle Military Academy in Bell Buckle, Tennessee, from which he frequently ran away. He fought in the Spanish-American War, and by the time he and Edwina married, in 1907, he was a fast-living traveling salesman in love with his life on the road, which mixed the bonhomie of his drinking, card-playing companions with the attentions of what were then called "light ladies." It is hard to imagine a worse match: the genteel, puritanical Edwina and the boisterous, alcoholic, quick-tempered C. C. Throughout his life, Williams was aware of an inner struggle between these two inherited aspects of his nature, and it would be many years before he succeeded in integrating them in his work.

Williams was the family's second child. His sister, Rose, was born in 1909. Throughout their years in the South they were inseparable; their nurse called them "the couple." A third child, Walter Dakin (called Dakin throughout his life) was born in 1919.

When Williams was six, the family moved to Clarksdale, Mississippi, in the region called the Mississippi Delta, where his grandfather took over the troubled Episcopal parish. The whole family took up residence in the handsome rectory of St. George's Episcopal Church on Sharkey Avenue. In 1916, Tom became ill with diphtheria, which almost killed him. While he recovered, his mother read to him from Dickens and Shakespeare, and as he gradually explored Shakespeare's plays himself, he found that he was drawn — not surprisingly for a young boy — more to the excitement of *Titus Andronicus* than to the philosophical speculations of *Hamlet* or *King Lear*. *Titus*'s bloody, high melodramatics made a permanent impression. They would stay with him for years, and for a long time, according to disapproving critics, would remain a constant in his work.

C. C.'s visits home from the road were often traumatic affairs. He considered Tom a sissy and displayed little interest in Rose. To the children, his presence was gigantic and threatening, and Williams never forgot the sounds that emanated from his parents' bedroom when his father demanded his conjugal rights from the reluctant Edwina. It's not surprising that Williams grew up with an ambivalent attitude toward sex, which is reflected in many works, among them the one-act *27 Wagons Full of Cotton*. In it, a young woman named Flora is both ashamed of and excited by the rough sex she has with her husband, Jake, and with Silva, the manager of a neighboring plantation.

In 1918, C. C.'s employer, the International Shoe Company, took him off his traveling route and promoted him to a desk job at its headquarters in St. Louis. That July, the family relocated north, ending Williams' idyllic childhood and introducing him to a city he quickly came to hate. Later, he would refer it to as "that cold city in the North" and "St. Pollution." However, this huge, crowded, noisy, and, to a child of seven, frightening place provided him with the stark setting of what became his first successful play, *The Glass Menagerie*.

As Rose approached adolescence, the family began to note transformations in her personality. Her natural good spirits were coming to resemble hysteria. At the same time, the extroverted girl turned into a withdrawn and taciturn young woman. In the next several years her behavior became increasingly erratic and disturbing. She would hide herself in the house for days at a time; she threatened her father with violence. Finally, she was institutionalized in 1937. She was diagnosed as having "dementia praecox," or schizophrenia. In 1943 she underwent a prefrontal lobotomy. The operation brought an end to her ravings and delusions, but also doomed her to a life of institutionalization and permanent exile from the world that existed outside of her damaged mind.

The effect of his sister's illness on Williams can't be overestimated. In his late adolescence, Williams was terrified that he, too, would go mad (and indeed, that fear never left him). He suffered from what he called in his journals "Blue devils," periods of deep depression that afflicted him throughout his life. In the summer of 1937 he wrote in his notebook, "Am I losing my mind? [...] — feel trapped tonight — frightened — have taken a sleeping pill but little effect — if only I had something definite to do with myself I might save myself. Well I am not going to give up the fight yet." It's important to notice that while was he was frequently convinced that he would end up like his sister, he just as frequently fought against that feeling. In the fall of the following year, he wrote, "And then there is always the shadow of what happened to Rose!" But the next day he added, "I want to live, live, live!!"

Rose was, without doubt, the most important person in his life, and images of her appear throughout his work, almost from the beginning to the very end. She appears in guises that reflect Williams' love and concern, but there are also darker images of her that suggest much more ambivalent feelings. On one hand, he developed a guilt for using her tragic life as material for his work (the way people use other people to further their own ends became an important theme in his work); on the other, his later plays also suggest an unconscious resentment of this guilt.

In 1929, Williams enrolled at the University of Missouri,

intending to major in journalism. The interest in journalism didn't last; he was drawn instead to the theater department. His grades were mostly low, and he flunked his Reserve Officer Training Course. In anger, his father refused to pay the tuition for his senior year. Instead, C. C. put Williams to work in the warehouse of the International Shoe Company as a clerk-typist, where he worked for three years. The move temporarily derailed Williams' college career but had significant implications for his future. At the warehouse, Williams had emotional experiences that would be directly reflected in *The Glass Menagerie*. These were unhappy years for Williams. Trapped in a job he hated, he felt free only at night when, fuelled by multiple cups of black coffee, he wrote poems and short stories in his attic bedroom, often until dawn. His desperation and the feeling of claustrophobia brought about by the job eventually drove him to a nervous breakdown in 1935. This gave him an excuse to quit the warehouse and return part-time to college. In 1938, Williams finally obtained a degree, from the theater department of the University of Iowa.

At the end of that year, at the age of twenty-seven, he left home never to return for more than a few days. He embarked on a life of restless travel, rarely remaining anywhere for very long. His first destination was New Orleans, where he hoped to get a job on the Federal Writer's Project, one of the many government programs created to reduce unemployment during the Great Depression. En route, he entered a playwriting contest sponsored by the Group Theatre, submitting four one-act plays grouped under the title *American Blues* and two full-length plays, *Candles to the Sun* and *Spring Storm*. Since the contest rules stipulated that entrants could be no more than twenty-five years old, Williams claimed that he was born in 1914, and perhaps to cover his tracks signed his name "Tennessee Williams." He didn't win the contest's $500 first prize, but he was awarded a special $100 prize for the one-acts and acquired a powerful agent, Audrey Wood. Shortly after this, he was awarded a $1,000 Rockefeller Fellowship. His career had begun.

THE SOUTH

The South shaped Williams' imagination as much as the particulars of his family life. His earliest years were spent there, and he absorbed its atmosphere, the nature of the land, the sounds of its language, and the customs of its people, creating out of them a personal geography where he set the majority of his plays and stories. Two parts of the South, in particular, dominate his work: the Mississippi Delta and New Orleans, while the Gulf Coast of Mississippi also figures in some of his major works. His plays and stories are studded with the names of locations and people well known to the local population in the Delta, who did not always take kindly to Williams' use of them in his work. Among the plays that Williams set in the Delta are *Spring Storm*, *27 Wagons Full of Cotton*, *Cat on a Hot Tin Roof*, *The Seven Descents of Myrtle*, *The Last of My Solid Gold Watches*, *Summer and Smoke*, *The Unsatisfactory Supper*, and *Orpheus Descending*.

The region referred to as the Delta isn't the place where the Mississippi empties into the Gulf of Mexico. Rather, the Delta is a large alluvial plain extending from Memphis, Tennessee, in the north to Yazoo City, Mississippi, in the south. Its western border is formed by the Mississippi and Yazoo Rivers, its eastern edge is the Choctaw Ridge, the beginning of the Mississippi hill country. Some of the richest soil in the South is found here, having been nourished over the centuries by the floods of the Mississippi River. The Delta is a great, flat fertile crescent, once dominated by huge cotton plantations, and cotton remains a major force in the region's economy. The population is diverse; in *Tennessee Williams and the South*, Kenneth Holditch lists not only the descendants of British settlers from North and South Carolina and Virginia and a large black population descended from slaves, but also Greeks, Lebanese, Italians, and Chinese.

The Delta is suffused with music, and the blues are ubiquitous. As Giles Oakley relates in *The Devil's Music: A History of the Blues*, "There were blues played in just about every circumstance; on the plantations, in shacks and house parties, in the streets, in the taverns and joints, in the cotton centers like Greenville, Greenwood, Yazoo City or Clarksdale, up to Memphis, or across the river into Arkansas…" Williams imbibed their rhythms just as he had those of the Bible and Shakespeare. The rich sounds and cadences of the inhabitants' speech found their way into Williams' work, too; all these contribute to the rich musicality that is the hallmark of his language.

Like William Faulkner, Williams was of at least two minds about the South. On one hand, it was a world of grace and charm. He knew that gracious world through his mother and maternal grandparents; he observed it in the life at the church rectories where the family lived before coming north, and from the visits he'd make with his grandfather when the Reverend Dakin called on his parishioners. The South — and the Delta in particular — is famous for the easygoing nature of its population and their culture. On the other hand, Williams observed that the Delta, especially, could also be a close-minded place where population closed ranks against newcomers and outsiders. It was a place where violence could erupt with lethal suddenness, especially for the black population. Williams summed up this attitude when he wrote, as quoted in Holditch and Leavitt, that it was "out of regret for a South that no longer exists that I write of the forces that destroyed it." The small-mindedness and xenophobia that could also be found in the Delta is one of Williams' subjects in *Battle of Angels* and *Orpheus Descending*, where outsiders such as Myra, Lady, and Val Xavier, and even insiders such as Carol Cutrere and Vee Talbot, are persecuted and even killed simply because they are different. Williams' most authoritative biographer, Lyle Leverich, points out that Clarksdale and its inhabitants provided the material for many characters and settings throughout Williams' career.

> Just as another southern writer, William Faulkner, had staked out nearby Sardis and Oxford, Mississippi as his Yokna-patawpha County, so Tennessee Williams would claim a circle of some twenty miles around Clarksdale as his literary

territory. Clarksdale would be renamed Blue Mountain, and a gambling club near Lula would be called Moon Lake Casino. Actual names like the Alcazar Hotel, Friars Point, Lyon, Tutwiler, Coahoma County, the Sunflower River and Moon Lake would figure in a number of his plays and stories.

When Williams returned to the South in 1938, however, it wasn't the small towns of the Delta that he had known in childhood that drew him. His destination was New Orleans. New Orleans is unique among American cities, and its differences are accentuated in the French Quarter, where Williams settled. Oliver Evans put it this way in *New Orleans*:

> There is a certain unreality about the French Quarter, as there is about Venice: it has the quality of a permanent illusion. This . . . has something to do with the extravagance of the architecture (so unlike any other in the United States) and something also to do with the peculiarly luminous quality of the light in New Orleans, and with the river mists that tend to overhang this part of the city, giving a mysterious and mirage-like appearance to its buildings. The French Quarter is like a dream framed by a fig tree — by such a tree, for instance, as grows, or used to grow, in the courtyard of the old Café Lafitte on Bourbon and St. Philip.

The smells, the sounds (especially the music), the diversity of the population all reminded Williams of the Delta, but magnified several times. Williams reflected this in the description of the setting, in the French Quarter, of *A Streetcar Named Desire*:

> *It is the first dark of an evening in early May. The sky that shows around the dim white building is a peculiarly tender blue, almost a turquoise, which invests the scene with a kind of lyricism and gracefully attenuates the atmosphere of decay. You can almost feel the warm breath of the brown river beyond the river warehouses*

with their faint redolences of bananas and coffee. A corresponding
air is evoked by the music of Negro entertainers at a barroom
around the corner. In this part of New Orleans you are practically
always just around the corner, or a few doors down the street, from
a tinny piano being played with the infatuated fluency of brown
fingers. This "blue piano" expresses the spirit of the life which goes
on here.

While the adult Williams rarely spent more than three weeks in
any one place, he returned to New Orleans often and bought a house
there. He also had one in Key West, Florida, but New Orleans,
specifically the French Quarter (also called the Vieux Carré), was his
spiritual home and his favorite city in America. In 1958 he told an
interviewer (see Devlin's collection of interviews),

> If I can be said to have a home, it is in New Orleans where I
> have lived off and on since 1938 and which has provided me
> with more material than any other part of the country. I live
> near the main street of the Quarter which is named Royal.
> Down the street, running on the same tracks, are two street-
> cars, one named Desire and the other named Cemetary.
> Their indiscouragable progress up and down Royal struck me
> as having some symbolic bearing of a broad nature on the life
> of the Vieux Carré —and everywhere else, for that matter.

The material that he found there frequently had to do with the
conflict between spirit and flesh. He said of the city, "I found the
kind of freedom I had always needed. And the shock of it against the
Puritanism of my nature has given me a theme, which I have never
ceased exploiting."

His earliest years in New Orleans were desperate. Devoting
himself to writing, he rarely took other jobs. He often had to pawn his
typewriter. But the richness of the life there, so different from the
oppressiveness he had felt in St. Louis, was liberating. It could also be
anxiety provoking. His first stay, in early 1939, lasted a scant two

months. The unbuttoned, frankly sexual atmosphere of Mardi Gras proved too daunting for that Puritanism of his nature; with a friend he struck out for the West Coast. It seems likely that the atmosphere of the Vieux Carré was bringing the truth of his homosexuality into his consciousness and he wasn't prepared for it. By the time he returned in 1941, however, he was quite prepared. While the ambivalence toward sex of any sort that had been ground into his psyche in his childhood never left him, he found great pleasure in the diversions that the French Quarter had to offer in that direction. Sex of every variety, for money and for free, was easily had in the Quarter, which led Oliver Evans to remark, "In New Orleans, you are always hearing people say that the French Quarter, while it might be interesting and convenient as a place to live, is no place in which to bring up children."

Like the Delta, New Orleans was fertile ground for Williams' imagination. *A Streetcar Named Desire*; *Suddenly Last Summer*; *The Lady of Larkspur Lotion*; *Lord Byron's Love Letter*; *Auto-Da-Fé*; *Mister Paradise*; *Thank You, Kind Spirit* and *And Tell Sad Stories of the Deaths of Queens* . . . are set there, among other works.

INFLUENCES: CRANE, CHEKHOV, AND LAWRENCE

When asked who influenced him most, Williams often cited three writers: the American poet Hart Crane, the Russian playwright and storywriter Anton Chekhov, and the English novelist D. H. Lawrence.

When Williams was a student at Washington University in St. Louis, he "liberated" a volume of poems by Hart Crane from the University library, and the book was a constant companion throughout his life and endless travels. Williams demonstrated his affinity with Crane by quoting Crane's work as epigraphs to his plays, including *A Streetcar Named Desire*, *Sweet Bird of Youth*, *Will Mr. Merriwether Return from Memphis?*, and the title of *Summer and Smoke*. Late in life he wrote a one-act about Crane and his mother, *Steps Must be Gentle*, which takes place at the bottom of the sea after Crane's suicide. Crane, along with Rimbaud, Williams wrote, was a poet who "touched fire that burned [him] alive," and in both Crane's and Williams' work one is struck by the power and intensity with which they transmute experience into art. One can easily see this subjectivity and intensity in Williams' writing, not in Crane's dense, difficult language, but in the accessible, more immediate working out of his characters' destinies by violence, fire, flood, and apocalypse.

It may be, however, that Crane's influence was as much biographical as literary as Gilbert Debusscher points out in "Minting Their Separate Wills," in Bloom's *Modern Critical Views: Tennessee Williams*:

> Williams was aware . . . of the truly stunning similarity of his and Crane's formative years, family situations, and aspirations. Crane's small-town origins, his family life, torn between egotistical parents who turned him into the battlefield of their marital strife; his fervent attachment to both his neurotic mother (with whom he was later to fall out) and his indulgent, doting grandmother; his early aversion to and later reconciliation with a father who opposed his aspirations as a poet and insisted he enter the family business; the bohemian wander-lust that prevented him from settling down permanently; his bouts of ill health which were often psychosomatic in origin; and finally his uphill fight for artistic integrity in an uncomprehending world, his torment by spells of self-doubt and despair . . . [and] a sexuality unfocused but predominantly homoerotic, were traits of Crane's life and personality in which Williams must have recognized himself as in a mirror.

Debusscher also points out that some of Williams' archetypal figures, particularly the doomed artist and the wandering poet, can be seen as images of Crane, whom Williams referred to as the "voyager-poet."

In 1939, before Williams wrote any of his major works, he wrote his agent Audrey Wood, "I have only one major theme for all my work which is the destructive impact of society on the sensitive, non-conformist individual." The empathetic side of Williams' nature had only to respond to the suffering he witnessed in St. Louis during the Great Depression and in the many popular socially conscious films he saw. The theme was certainly reinforced in him in 1935 when he began reading Chekhov, whose work shares this theme.

Several critics have pointed out similarities and affinities between *The Glass Menagerie* and *The Seagull* (an artistic son who cannot communicate with his mother, whom he alternately loves and is stifled by) and *A Streetcar Named Desire* and *The Cherry Orchard* (the depiction of the death of an attenuated way of life, personified by Blanche DeBois and Madame Ranevskya, and the rise of a new, vital life in the persons of Stanley Kowlaski and Lopakhin). Williams was also influenced by Chekhov's unorthodox dramatic structure, which relied on the accumulation of many small moments for its effect rather than the traditional one or two large, pivotal moments. This became Williams' structure, too, and it can be found in *The Strangest Kind of Romance*, *The Glass Menagerie*, *The Night of the Iguana*, *Small Craft Warnings*, and *Something Cloudy, Something Clear*, among other plays.

Writers often admire in their colleagues the qualities that are the opposite of their own, and Williams strived to achieve a Chekhovian coolness and objectivity that came to him with difficulty. In *The Night of the Iguana*, Williams gives to Hannah Jelkes, the itinerate artist, a credo that describes Chekhov's own attitude: "I don't judge people, I draw them." He certainly achieves a sense of objectivity at the end of *The Glass Menagerie*. After seven scenes of conflict and misunderstandings between Tom and Amanda, the image of her that Williams leaves us with is this: *We see, as though through soundproof glass, that Amanda appears to be making a comforting speech to Laura, who is huddled upon the sofa. Now that we cannot hear the mother's speech, her silliness is gone and she has dignity and tragic beauty.*

D. H. Lawrence was another important influence early in Williams' career, although in later years, as the values he emphasized in his work underwent a profound change, Williams himself dismissed it. Certainly, what's clear in much of his work through 1962 is an identification with Lawrence's "belief in the purity of sensual life, the purity and the beauty of it," as he said in an interview (see Devlin). As Gilbert Debusscher, referencing the work of Norman J. Fedder, puts it in an essay called "Creative Rewriting: European and American Influences on the Dramas of Tennessee Williams" (in *The Cambridge Companion to Tennessee Williams*):

> Williams was attracted to Lawrence because of the Englishman's emphasis on sexuality: to him, sex was a means of restoring the balance between the two antagonistic forces of the flesh and the spirit, locked in a battle in which the British writer felt the intellect had dangerously gained the upper hand. Sex was also to be a liberating force opposed to the bourgeois Puritanism of the Victorian Age and of the American Genteel Tradition. As its apostle, Lawrence was part of a larger movement of liberation — social, political as well as emotional – born in the wake of Freudianism. It is therefore entirely possible that William's [sic] own insistence on the importance of sex derives as much from Lawrence as from the emerging Freudian revolution of which the playwright was to become a leading proponent on Broadway.

When he was young, Williams was enamored enough of Lawrence and his philosophy, as he understood it, to write two one-acts that featured him: *I Rise in Flame, Cried the Phoenix*, about Lawrence's last hours, and *Adam and Eve on the Ferry*, a comedy in which Lawrence gives advice to a lovelorn young woman. Another early one-act, *The Case of the Crushed Petunias*, was inspired by Lawrence's story, "The Fox." Collaborating with Donald Windham, he dramatized a

Lawrence short story, "You Touched Me," which had a brief run on Broadway in 1945 (with an exclamation mark added at the end of title).

For Williams, sex was not merely a pleasant pastime or a way to propagate the race. It was a life force that opposed life and vitality against everything that militated against them, from soul-killing daily habit to small-mindedness, Puritanism, and bigotry. In *Battle of Angels* and *Orpheus Descending*, the life force is personified in Val Xavier, while Jabe Torrance and his men represent death-in-life. In *The Rose Tattoo*, Alvaro Mangiacavallo reawakens the spirit in Sarafina Della Rosa; Maggie tries to cure her husband, Brick's, spiritual paralysis through sex and love in *Cat on a Hot Tin Roof*. In *A Streetcar Named Desire*, Stanley Kowalski is another version of the life force, and a demonstration of what Lawrence called "blood consciousness": a knowledge that exists independently of what he referred to as "mental and nerve consciousness."

Lawrence also was interested in finding a proper balance between the love of oneself and of another, between what he called the "separatist" mode and the "sympathetic" mode. One must find, in other words, a balance between self-love (the "separatist" mode) and the love of others (the "sympathetic" mode). Williams may not necessarily have read Lawrence's *Psychoanalysis and the Unconscious*, where this division is so explicit, but he echoed it in work after work, because he sensed in himself an instinct to serve his own needs before those of other people. Also, although he identified strongly with Lawrence's belief in sex as a liberating force, he was ambivalent about it, and in several plays he showed that love and sex are snares, trapping his characters in punishment and even death.

To this list of influences can be added other writers, including Eugene O'Neill and August Strindberg, from whom Williams gained a tragic sense and also the realization that styles such as Expressionism were better suited than material realism for the depiction of heightened emotion. He admired the lyrical intensity of Federico García Lorca, the toughness and frankness of Genet, and later came to share Harold Pinter's sense of the sinister and mysterious and Samuel Beckett's vision of a static world that could best be reflected in a mixture of the comic and the tragic.

APPRENTICE PLAYS

By 1938, Williams had completed four long plays. He later described them as "coarse, juvenile and talky," but they are better than that, and they contain the seeds of much of his later work. *Candles to the Sun* (1936) is about the lives of coal miners in Alabama. On the one hand, it is a plea for social justice and communal solidarity on behalf of men and women who live with poverty and disease. It is also a record of a family divided by temperament, education, and a vision of a freer future. *The Fugitive Kind* (1937) is set in a St. Louis flophouse by the Mississippi River, peopled by hobos, mobsters, and the desperate poor caught in the economic vise of the times. Like *Candles to the Sun* (and *The Glass Menagerie* and *A Streetcar Named Desire*), it centers on a family whose members have vastly different aspirations, who, if they were to remain under one roof, would frequently find themselves in conflict. *Not About Nightingales* (1938) exemplifies one of the primary themes of Williams' mature work: the desire to flee a confining situation. It could not be more starkly expressed than it is in the setting for this play: a penitentiary in which prisoners are tortured in the "Klondike," a cell where the temperature reaches over 125 degrees. All these plays are demands for social justice. Still, although he drew plots from other peoples' lives (*Candles to the Sun* and *Not About Nightingales* were based in part on newspaper stories), his characters' desperation to escape their constraining situations, their yearnings for freedom and a better life, were expressions of Williams' own desires.

These plays also demonstrate another important influence on Williams: the movies. Williams was the first major American playwright, in fact, to be so influenced by film. His early plays were informed by the social content of many of the movies of the thirties, but film's influence on Williams' *form* lasted his entire career. The fluid way in which film moves from scene to scene, its use of visual as well as literary images, are reflected in Williams' work at least as early as *Not About Nightingales* and can be found in plays at every stage of his career.

In her excellent introductions to the published texts of *The Fugitive Kind* and *Not About Nightingales*, Allean Hale outlines the effects that the films of that era had on him. He drew much of the language of these plays from the short, sharp, streetwise dialogue of the movies, and borrowed aspects of their plots, as well. Then he added to them the lengthy aria-like speeches, with long, lyrical rhythms, that were his own invention.

He was also aware of the new plays with social themes, particularly those produced by the Group Theatre and its members, including Irwin Shaw's *Bury the Dead* (1935) and Clifford Odets's *Waiting for Lefty*, *Awake and Sing*, and *Paradise Lost* (all 1935). Williams' fourth apprentice play, *Spring Storm* (1937–38) was less concerned with social justice and in all ways is a much more personal play. It is the first play Williams set in the Delta, and is a lyrical statement about the longings of four young people to escape their physical or emotional situations, the courage that it takes to do so, and the social and psychological forces arrayed against them. In all four apprentice plays, Williams already found ways to express his "one major theme" using a contemporary, populist language suffused with personal, but accessible, imagery.

THE BROADWAY THEATER AS WILLIAMS FOUND IT

The Broadway theater that Williams found when he moved to New York in 1940 was similar to the one that greeted Eugene O'Neill more than two decades earlier. Broadway (which, with only a small handful of exceptions, *was* the American professional theater) was in business to earn a profit, and, unless productions of serious plays featured stars, they usually did not make money (indeed, it is not very different today). Broadway was dominated by light romantic comedies, melodramas, and musicals. The biggest hit that year was *Arsenic and Old Lace*.

The basic style was photographic, or material, realism, which showed characters living in a world that looked, sounded, and operated exactly like the audience's. Its high priest had been the producer, director, and playwright David Belasco (1853–1931). For his play *The Governor's Lady* (1912), he re-created exactly, down to the napkins and silverware, Child's Restaurant, which each night provided the food that the actors ate onstage. For *Madame Butterfly* (1900) he created a lighting sequence lasting twelve minutes that represented the passage of the night from sunset to dawn. Belasco set the production style that nearly everyone on Broadway followed.

There were, however, two significant producing organizations that veered from typical Broadway content and style to various degrees: the Theatre Guild and the Group Theatre. The intention of Theatre Guild, founded in 1918, which produced on Broadway and toured nationally, was to elevate the kinds of plays produced in New York. It produced the work of important international playwrights such as Luigi Pirandello, George Bernard Shaw, Sean O'Casey, and August Strindberg. The Guild also produced plays by American writers such as Sidney Howard, William Saroyan, Maxwell Anderson, and Robert Sherwood. It was perhaps most famous for being the Broadway home of Eugene O'Neill, the first American playwright to aspire to make the American theater as important as that of Europe. In many plays, O'Neill defied Belasco's realism by employing devices such as masks, internal monologues, and Expressionistic sets and lighting. The Guild was a middlebrow endeavor that believed in the elevating nature of culture as such and usually relied on stars to bring in audiences. Nevertheless, it was an important and powerful institution that produced many plays that otherwise would not have been seen either on Broadway or in the several cities across the country where it brought its touring productions.

The Group Theatre, founded in 1931 by three employees of the Theatre Guild, has proven to be the most influential theater company in American history. Its founders, Harold Clurman, Cheryl Crawford, and Lee Strasberg, were devoted to building an acting company that performed plays that spoke with immediacy and urgency, but that also would, as Clurman wrote in his memoir of the Group Theatre, *The Fervent Years*, "link the actor as an individual with the creative purpose of the playwright." Most crucially, Clurman said, "our interest in the life of our times must lead us to the discovery of those methods that would most truly convey this life through the theatre." The Group members shared the same aesthetic values and trained together using a method devised by Lee Strasberg based on Stanislavski's "system." The goal was to find each character's moment-to-moment specific emotional, intellectual truth and connect it to the meaning of the play as a whole. The Group was best known for its productions of plays by Clifford Odets, the most famous of which was *Waiting for Lefty*, which, while not officially a Group production, featured its actors and was written under the Group's auspices.

The Group lasted only nine years, but its importance is immeasurable, for Williams' career as well as for the American theater. Beyond awarding him the $100 special prize in its contest (an unheard-of sum for the chronically broke young Williams) and effectively beginning his career outside St. Louis, it provided him with models of new kinds of theatrical voices: the urgent social protests of Clifford Odets fashioned in a street *patois* that aspired (perhaps too self-consciously) to art; and the verve and spontaneity of William Saroyan (who was also produced by the Theatre Guild).

The Group Theatre also provided Williams with actors capable of performing his work. When it folded in 1939, three members — Cheryl Crawford, Elia Kazan, and Robert Lewis — went on to found the Actors Studio, a place where working actors could continue their training. It soon came to be dominated by Lee Strasberg and his actor-training techniques that became known as the Method. Kazan later would direct *A Streetcar Named Desire* using a number of actors who studied at the Studio, including Karl Malden and Kim Hunter. Kazan went on to direct *Camino Real*, *Cat on a Hot Tin Roof*, and *Sweet Bird of Youth*, while Crawford produced *The Rose Tattoo*, *Camino Real*, *Sweet Bird of Youth*, and *Period of Adjustment*. Another Group alumna, Stella Adler, also became an influential teacher. One of her students was Marlon Brando, who would star in the Broadway production and film version of *A Streetcar Named Desire*. Clurman would direct the national company of *Streetcar* and the Broadway production of *Orpheus Descending*; as a critic, he was a steadfast defender of Williams' work. More important than these personal relationships, however, was the fact that the Theatre Guild, and even more so the Group Theatre, created the kind of climate on Broadway in which a noncommercial playwright like Williams, who wasn't interested in the kind of photographic realism that audiences were familiar with, could exist.

Two movements that also played important parts in laying the groundwork for productions of Williams' plays were the Little Theater movement and the New Stagecraft. The Little Theater movement began at the beginning of the twentieth century as a response to the commercialism of the New York theater. It took its inspiration from the private theatres in Europe that operated as clubs rather than public theaters, and thus avoided censorship. These theaters produced plays by August Strindberg, Henrik Ibsen, Gerhardt Hauptmann, and other path-breaking playwrights. These new American theaters sprang up in New York and in cities around the country. Some of them, including the Cleveland Play House and the Pasadena Playhouse, would later be among the first to produce Williams' plays. In New York, the most important Little Theaters were the Provincetown Players, which first produced O'Neill, and the Washington Square Players, from which the Theatre Guild emerged.

The New Stagecraft movement was allied to the Little Theaters. It was primarily a movement of young American stage designers who saw in the radical designs of Europeans such as

Adolph Appia and Edward Gordon Craig evocative, poetic alternatives to the Belasco-style realism that dominated the American theater. This group included Robert Edmond Jones, Lee Simonsen, Norman Bel Geddes, and Jo Mielziner. Mielziner would design sets and lights for six of Williams' plays: *The Glass Menagerie*, *A Streetcar Named Desire*, *Summer and Smoke*, *Cat on a Hot Tin Roof*, *Sweet Bird of Youth*, and *Period of Adjustment*. Because these two movements provided a mindset and group of directors and designers who not only understood Williams' more poetic approach to the theater but also helped him realize it, both proved vital to Williams' success.

WILLIAMS' "PLASTIC THEATER"

In terms of the lyricism of Williams' language and the nonrealistic approach to design taken by Mielziner, Broadway had not seen a play like *The Glass Menagerie* before, and its success was immediate: It played 563 performances, and two national companies toured the country. Williams wrote four pages of production notes to accompany the published play, in which he outlined the way the play should look — and the way it shouldn't: "The straight realistic play," he declared, "with its genuine Frigidaire and authentic ice cubes [. . .] has the same virtue of a photographic likeness." The theater, however, ought to be concerned with poetic truth, which can only be represented through the transforming power of metaphor, suggestion, and imagination: the "plastic theatre which must take the place of the exhausted theatre of realistic conventions."

To this end, Mielziner designed a set that relied as much, if not more, on lighting than on three-dimensional pieces, and those pieces would often dissolve through the use of translucent materials to create a world of memory and imagination. This lent the play a cinematic feel. One of Williams' non-naturalistic conventions, however, was not used. For every scene he had written titles that were meant to be projected; images within scenes were also occasionally called for. Williams meant them to underscore the important points or themes in each scene. The producers, however, didn't see their purpose and refused to pay for them, and so they weren't used (and to this day are omitted from the acting edition of the script).

Williams' interest in a less materially realistic kind of theater can be traced at least as far back as *The Fugitive Kind*, in which he describes a set with an expressionistic function:

> *A large glass window admits a skyline of the city whose towers are outlined at night by a faint electric glow, so that we are always conscious of the city as a great implacable force, pressing in upon the shabby room and crowding its fugitive inhabitants back against their last wall. . . .*

> *When lighted the set is realistic. But during the final scenes of the play, where the mood is predominantly lyrical, the realistic details are lost — the great window, the red light on the landing and the shadow walls make an almost expressionistic background.*

Expressionism is a style in which all the elements of a production, including the text, acting, set, lighting, and even costume design, are meant to externalize the characters' internal emotional lives. Williams most likely learned it from plays he read while a student at the University of Missouri, including O'Neill's *The Hairy Ape* and Strindberg's later works. Artists tend to use the tools that most accurately reproduce the world as they experience it, and the important point is that Williams responded to these playwrights' Expressionism and adopted it himself because it was the most direct, efficient way to record his almost perpetually heightened inner state. He gravitated to it naturally as a way of re-creating the world as he knew it.

It wasn't only the physical production that made *The Glass Menagerie* memorable, however. It was the lyrical sound of the text itself, and Williams' embrace of a Chekhovian kind of storytelling. In an introduction to the 2004 edition of *A Streetcar Named Desire*, Arthur Miller wrote of *The Glass Menagerie*:

> Seeing it was like stumbling on a flower in a junkyard. . . its lines were fluid and idiomatic but at the same time rhythmically composed. Playwriting . . . was at the time regarded as something close to engineering, structure and its problems taking first place in all considerations of the art. *Menagerie* appeared to have no structure . . . It was still a time when the convention was to suspect Chekhov's plays as real drama because in them "nothing happened." Of course it was all a question of emphasis; the Broadway play emphasized plot, while Williams had pushed language and character to the front of the stage as never before, in America, anyway.

THE NEED TO FLEE VERSUS THE URGE TO REMAIN

Williams was a man divided against himself in several ways, and he was aware of this from an early age. In 1936 he wrote in his notebook, "If only I could realize I am not 2 persons. I am only one. There is no sense in this division. An enemy inside myself! How absurd!" Twenty years later, after much fame and success, he wrote to his friend Maria St. Just, "One's enemy is always part of oneself." This division expressed itself through two major themes that appear in his work from the first apprentice plays written in the 1930s through the end of his career: the urge to flee versus the urge to stay, and the need to reveal vs. the urge to conceal.

Two months before leaving home for New Orleans, Williams wrote in his notebook, "Now is the time to make a break — get away, away — I have pinned pictures of wild birds on my lavatory screen — Significant — I'm desperately anxious to escape." This anxiety reveals a spiritual and physical claustrophobia that afflicted Williams throughout his life. Desperation is an important word in considering Williams' characters. What they want, they want desperately, and nowhere is this more true than in the conflict they feel between the need for love, which will only be found if they stay with someone, and the equally desperate need to flee, to be free from the constraints placed on them by others. Images of birds are a constant throughout his work. As Gore Vidal pointed out in the introduction to Williams' *Collected Stories*, "The image of the bird is everywhere [in Williams' work]. The bird is flight, poetry, life. The bird is time, death." In *Orpheus Descending*, the traveling musician, Val — who hates to be tied down and believes that each person is, finally, alone in his own skin — tells Lady Torrance, the woman he will fall in love with:

> You know, there's a kind of bird that don't have legs so it can't light on nothing but has to stay all its life on its wings in the sky? [. . .] But those little birds, they don't have no legs at all and they live their whole lives on the wing, and they sleep on the wind, that's how they sleep at night, they just spread their wings and go to sleep on the wind [. . .] [and] never light on this earth but one time when they die!

Lady, trapped in a loveless marriage with the man whose Ku Klux Klan–like mob killed her father, is dubious; "I don't think nothing living has ever been that free, not even nearly," she says.

Birds also represent sex, which is both a coming together and a flight from the world of repression and oppression, from the people whom Williams called "the squares." In *Camino Real*, the Baron de Charlus, out cruising for sex with another man, hopes to find the "canaries [that] sing in your bedsprings after midnight."

The urge to flee is amply demonstrated in one of Williams' best plays, the one that first brought him great recognition, *The Glass Menagerie*. The plot is simple — so simple in fact that a number of critics have written (incorrectly) that it's a play in which nothing happens. It takes place in St. Louis during the Depression. A family of three — the mother, Amanda Wingfield; and two children in their twenties, Laura and Tom — struggle to make ends meet. The family's desperate economic circumstances are due to the fact that Mr. Wingfield fled many years ago; a reminder of his flight and absence hangs prominently on the wall in the form of his portrait. The last the family heard from him was a postcard from Mexico, whose two words encapsulate the warring urges of this conflict: "Hello — Goodbye!"

Laura, who walks with a slight limp due to a childhood illness, has retreated into her own world, symbolized by a collection of small glass animals: She has fled inward. Tom works in a shoe warehouse but dreams of being a writer and of joining the merchant marines to see the world. His escape is both outward, away from the stifling confines of St. Louis, and inward, when, as a writer, he will rely on his imagination to make art out of his experience.

Amanda, who grew up a privileged young woman in the world of the old, genteel South, often reminisces, no doubt with some exaggeration, about her past. However, she hasn't the luxury of escaping her current circumstances; she confronts them directly. She works at several jobs and, concerned about Laura's future, tries to find her first a career and when that fails, a husband. At her urging, Tom brings home for dinner a young man from the warehouse named Jim O'Connor, but he turns out to be an unpromising gentleman caller for Laura: He has (he claims) a fiancée. On the heels of this disastrous dinner, Tom leaves home forever, but he can never leave the image of his sister behind.

Despite the play's reputation as a gentle memory play, Williams' description of the set tells us immediately that this is a world of desperation and struggle:

> *The Wingfield apartment in the rear of the building, one of those vast, hive-like conglomerations of cellular living units that flower as warty growths in the overcrowded urban centers of lower*

*middle-class population and are symptomatic of the impulse of this
largest and fundamentally enslaved section of American society to
avoid fluidity and differentiation and to exist and function as one
interfused mass of automatism.*

*The apartment faces an alley and is entered by a fire escape, a
structure whose name is a touch of accidental poetic truth, for all of
those huge buildings are burning with the slow and implacable fires
of human desperation. The fire escape is part of what we see — that
is, the landing of it and steps descending from it.*

Tom is imprisoned in this cramped apartment in which there is
no privacy and is desperate to find a way out. His only escape is into
his imagination when he reads and writes, and even then, Amanda
violates his privacy by confiscating his books (including one by D. H.
Lawrence), looking over his shoulder, and interfering when he tries to
write. At night he escapes to the movies and to places that remain
mysterious, staying out until the early hours of the morning.

Life away from the apartment is no less constricting and soul-
destroying: He labors in a shoe warehouse, where eventually he's fired
for writing poetry on the tops of shoe boxes. Once he saves enough
money, he escapes the family and joins the merchant marines, a job
that will allow him to roam the world and free him from the necessity
of settling down.

Although she may appear to be fragile, Laura is as strong and
resourceful as her mother and brother. Her mother wants her to
learn typing and stenography, but for months, unknown to Amanda,
she has skipped her classes at business school. Laura arranges her life
to do exactly as she wishes, which is to escape into the recesses of her
mind and imagination, polishing and caring for the animals in her
glass menagerie.

Jim, the gentleman caller, also has the urge to flee. In high
school, where he was popular and accomplished, everyone expected
him to go on to achieve great things. Now, six years later, he, too,

works in the shoe warehouse. Bent on escaping an ordinary life, he's taking a night-school class in public speaking and has made, he says, all the connections to get into television once the industry gets off the ground.

He's a charming character, but not, perhaps, altogether trust-worthy. He is greatly impressed with himself, and spouts endless bromides that sound as if they came from writers of self-improvement books, like Norman Vincent Peale. When Laura describes to him her precious glass menagerie, he's paying so little attention he has to ask, "What did you say — about glass?" Yet, callow though he is, after a gentle kiss, he is so touched by something in Laura that for the first time in the scene he becomes tongue-tied. When he regains his composure, he tells her that he wishes he had a sister like her. He also reveals that he's not in a position to "do the right thing": He is engaged to a girl named Betty. He quickly flees into the night.

Jim is often played as just a nice boy who, if he weren't engaged, would make the perfect husband for Laura. However, he is ambitious and more than a little self-centered. What he believes in is "the future of television." When he tells Laura that all he's waiting for is the business to get underway, Williams provides a stage direction: *His eyes are starry*. He tells her, "*Knowledge — Zzzzzp! Money — Zzzzzp! Power — Zzzzzp! That's the cycle democracy is built on!*" In the context of Williams' work, money and power are not values to prize as much as sensitivity, or freedom from the "vast hive-like conglomerations of cellular living-units" and the "interfused mass of automatism" that crush the individuality out of people. As Tom describes him, Jim is "an emissary from a world of reality" and "the most realistic character in the play." Neither of these is necessarily a compliment in the world of *The Glass Menagerie*. With all of Laura's many quirks, Jim would soon realize that she is not the woman he would want to take with him into executive suites on his rise up the corporate ladder.

Jim is not a bad person, just entirely unsuited for Laura. After they kiss, when he senses what is special about her and feels a sudden attraction, he mentions his engagement and beats a hasty retreat into the night. Does his fiancée even exist? Or is she an invention that allows Jim to escape without a commitment to calling again? The conflict in the Gentleman Caller scene is the result of Laura's own starry-eyed view of Jim, on whom she's had a crush since high school, and our own clear-eyed, objective opinion of him that we can draw based on his words and actions. The sadness in the scene is our realization that these two young people are unsuited for each other. It's possible to sense that Laura's way of recovering from this encounter will be to escape deeper into the comforting world of her glass menagerie.

This urge to flee is matched in Williams' work by the need to remain, out of love, empathy, or guilt, for the sake of another person. Characters are drawn back against their will to places they sense they must leave. The form of *The Glass Menagerie* suggests that Tom's attempt to flee his confinement has not been entirely successful: "The play is memory," he says. In his memory he revisits the apartment time and again; he can't let it go. The story he tells us is an attempt to escape the past: Perhaps through revisiting it and, as a writer, making art of it, he'll be able to let it go. His last speech tells us how unsuccessful his attempt at escape has been:

> I left St. Louis. I descended the steps of this fire escape for the last time and followed, from then on, in my father's footsteps, attempting to find in motion what was lost in space. I traveled around a great deal. The cities swept about me like dead leaves, leaves that were brightly colored but torn away from the branches. I would have stopped, but I was pursued by something. It always came upon me unawares, taking me altogether by surprise. Perhaps it was a familiar bit of music. Perhaps it was only a transparent piece of glass. Perhaps I am walking along a street at night, in some strange city before I have found companions. I pass the lighted window of a shop where perfume is sold. The window is

filled with pieces of colored glass, tiny transparent bottles in delicate colors, like bits of a shattered rainbow. Then all at once my sister touches my shoulder. I turn around and look into her eyes. Oh Laura, Laura, I tried to leave you behind me, but I am more faithful than I intended to be! I reach for a cigarette, I cross the street, I run into the movies or a bar, I buy a drink, I speak to the nearest stranger — anything that can blow your candles out! [. . .] For nowadays the world is lit by lightening! Blow out your candles, Laura — and so goodbye . . .

This will not be the last time that he tries to say good-bye to the image of his family. He may travel as far as his need to escape takes him, but in all likelihood they will follow him forever.

Sometimes in a Williams play, returning to someone out of love or empathy has fatal consequences. In *The Fugitive Kind*, a bank robber on the run, named Terry, has convinced Glory, who works in her father's flophouse, to run away with him to Mexico. They return to the flophouse for a moment, and in the brief time it takes for Terry to help Glory's intoxicated brother Leo into bed, the police arrive and kill him. In *Orpheus Descending*, the wandering singer Val Xavier stays in dangerous Two-River County longer than he intends because he has fallen in love with Lady Torrance. The result is death for both of them: Lady is shot by her dying husband, Jabe, and Val is burned to death by a mob. In *Sweet Bird of Youth*, Chance Wayne returns to his hometown on the Gulf Coast of Mississippi. Years earlier, he had given his girlfriend, Heavenly, a venereal disease and was ordered by her father, the powerful political kingpin Boss Finley, to leave and never return. When he does — to take Heavenly away with him in a half-baked scheme to become movie stars —the Boss's henchmen castrate him.

In Williams' plays, characters find themselves trapped in coal mines (*Candles to the Sun*), dead-end jobs (*The Glass Menagerie*), poverty and social injustice (*The Fugitive Kind*), prisons (*Not About*

Nightingales), and even in their own desires (*Suddenly Last Summer*). The worst trap, though, may be other people.

It is rare in a Williams' play that the coming together of two people is an altogether positive event. At first glance, *The Rose Tattoo* seems to be one of those plays: When Alvaro Mangiacavallo arrives in the small Gulf Coast town, Serafina Delle Rose is in double mourning: for her husband's death and for his marital betrayals while alive. Through love (and sex), Alvaro gives her back her life. There is even every indication that he, a traveling man who drives a truck, will settle down with her. However, this happy ending is shadowed by the relationship of Serafina's daughter Rosa and her rather reluctant suitor, Jack. Jack is a sailor — another restless young man who doesn't want to be tied down. The fifteen-year-old Rosa has been pursuing Jack throughout the play. A stage direction in Act One has her raining kisses on his face until he must forcefully pull himself away; at a dance at the high school gym he's alarmed at how sexually she dances with him. In Act Three, as he tries to part with her for the last time before returning to his ship, she threatens to follow him to the hotel where he's staying. She wants him to give her the gold ring he wears in his ear so that she can put it on her finger. The pivotal stage direction reads: *He breaks away and runs toward the road. From the foot of the steps he glares fiercely back at her like a tiger through the bars of a cage. She clings to the two porch pillars, her body leaning way out.* The stage direction suggests he is already feeling trapped. Rosa cries, "Look for me! I will be there!" Jack runs from the house, fleeing toward his freedom, determined not to be entangled.

In *A Streetcar Named Desire*, Stella and Stanley Kowalski are clearly in love, but this doesn't stop him from beating her when she's pregnant or from raping her sister, Blanche DuBois. Blanche is fleeing the long wreckage of her marriage to Allan Grey, the young man she had married many years before without knowing he was gay. Her cruel public exposure of his sexuality at Moon Lake Casino led to his suicide, and ever since, she has been trying to outrun the memory of that night.

One character in *Streetcar* who manages to avoid an entangling relationship is Mitch, Stanley's best friend. By the middle of the play he is eagerly courting Blanche. After she tells him the story of Allan Grey's death he recognizes in her a kindred spirit, a lonely soul, like his own. "You need somebody. And I need somebody, too," he says to her. "Could it be — you and me, Blanche?" It looks as though these two lonely people will find peace and contentment with each other.

By Scene Nine, however, Mitch has learned the truth about Blanche's past. She has tried to wipe the memory of Allan from her mind by an obsessive indulgence in sex: first with soldiers who are bivouacked outside her family home in Laurel, Mississippi, then with young men in a hotel, and finally with an underage high school student. Like Allan's, her sexual transgression is exposed, and she is forced to flee her home. After hearing all this, Mitch changes his mind. "You're not clean enough to bring in the house with my mother," he tells her, and walks out. He flees from the relationship he once sought, and Blanche, left alone again with her increasingly frightening memories and delusions, is raped by Stanley and goes mad.

As he grew older, Williams' pessimism about the ability of permanent relationships to make people happy only darkened. In *The Two-Character Play*, a brother and sister, Felice and Clare, are actors perpetually touring in a play that seems to be about their childhood. They are locked together in a permanent bond of love and loathing, and they cannot bear to be with each other, but they also can't endure the possibility of being alone. In *In the Bar of a Tokyo Hotel*, Mark and Miriam are trapped in a marriage fueled by torment and disdain that can end only in death.

If one doesn't commit oneself to other people, however, if one always flees from the possibility of love, what is left? In *Vieux Carré*, the old widowed landlady, Mrs. Wire, gives the answer to The Writer, a young innocent man about to embark on his career and life. "I'll tell you, there's so much loneliness in this house that you can hear it [. . .] groaning in the walls." For Williams, this is the tragedy of life: Combining your life with another person's leads to entrapment, unhappiness, possibly even death. To flee from human connections leaves one isolated and lonely. Here, too, death will be the endpoint.

Yet, it's important to point out that this urge to flee is, after all, only one side to the conflict. If the urge to flee is an expression of D. H. Lawrence's "separatist" love of oneself, it is always at odds with what he called the "sympathetic mode," the love of others. In the end, this is what draws Williams' characters back to those places that their need for self-preservation tells them to flee. For all of their arguing, the *Glass Menagerie*'s Wingfield family loves each other deeply. In *The Fugitive Kind*, Terry dies because he stops to help a helpless man. Val knows he runs a terrible risk by staying in Two-River County, but he does so because he loves Lady and because she needs him. Although Mitch deserts Stella, we don't know whether he will be able to live with his actions or be haunted by them. Williams gives us a hint, however, in a stage direction near the end of the play. When the doctor from the mental institution arrives to take Blanche away, Stanley's friends, who have gathered for the weekly poker game, look at the scene with curiosity. But Mitch *"keeps staring down at his hands on the table."* He can't bear to watch what's happened to the woman he hoped would bring an end to his loneliness. If the flights of Williams' characters are often unsuccessful, if they stay to take the chance of loving and being loved, then their humanity is triumphant, regardless of what becomes of their flesh.

THE RAVAGES OF TIME

In *Streetcar*, Blanche DuBois is fleeing many things; one of them is time. Time is the enemy of a great many of Williams' characters. It is a degrader and a destroyer of everything: of personal attractiveness, of gentility and civilization, of hopes and aspirations, of personal innocence. In an essay called "On a Streetcar Named Success,"

Williams wrote, "That time is short and it doesn't return again. It is slipping away while I write this and while you read it, and the monosyllable of the clock is Loss, loss, loss, unless you devote your heart to its opposition." In another essay, called "The Timeless World of a Play," he called it "the corrupting rush of time."

In *Streetcar*, Blanche flees Laurel, and throws herself on the mercy of her sister Stella and brother-in-law Stanley. She is offended by the way they live and by Stanley's uncouth ways. She calls him an ape and urges Stella to be better than he is, even if that means finding a man who represents the old values, a better time. She describes his violent poker party of the night before:

> His poker night! — you call it — this party of apes! Somebody growls — some creature snatches something — the fight is on! *God!* Maybe we are a long way from being made in God's image, but Stella — my sister — there has been *some* progress made since then! Such things as art — as poetry and music — such kinds of new light have come into the world since then! In some kinds of people some tenderer feelings have had some little beginning! That we have got to make *grow!* And *cling* to, and hold as our flag! In this dark march toward whatever it is we're approaching. . . . *Don't — don't hang back with the brutes!*

Many critics view Blanche as a representative of a kinder, gentler time and Stanley of the coarse, brutal reality of post-war America. Williams, though, is ambivalent. For all of her sensitivities and culture, Blanche is something of a snob and a liar. Her family's past is also represented by their home, Belle Reve, which was lost through their irresponsibility and corruption. The present is not represented only by Stanley, who is both brutish and tender, but also by the French Quarter, which is alive and full of vitality, energy, and all the sensual experiences Williams details in his description of the set.

Blanche herself has been corrupted by time, which has robbed her of youth. She will only let Mitch see her in shadows and at night, to hide her advancing age (although she is only in her thirties). Worse, she's become an exploiter of other people; she has used the young men she slept with to assuage her guilt about what happened to Allan. Indeed, perhaps the most terrible effect time has on the people in Williams' plays is the way it turns them into users of others.

Williams believed that, over time, we lose our innocence by becoming users of other people — lest we become used by them. Val tells Myra, ". . . there's just two kinds of people, the ones that are bought, and the buyers!" Williams' most thorough meditation on the users and the used is also one of his best, most concentrated plays, *Suddenly Last Summer*. The play is filled with metaphors for the ways in which people use each other in almost any relationship. In fact, the play suggests, there seems to be no relationship not based on using and being used. We devour our own; cannibalism is the way of the world.

The dead, offstage character Sebastian Venable, a poet so minor as to be unknown to anyone outside of his family, has been killed in a distant town called Cabeza de Lobo, perhaps in Mexico, devoured by a pack of poverty-stricken boys whom he had used for sex. Sebastian's exploitation of the boys and their shocking form of retribution, however, are merely the most obvious examples of the ways in which almost every living organism uses others for its own gain.

The play takes place in New Orleans, in the garden of Sebastian's Aunt Violet, a garden of Venus flytraps and "beasts, serpents and birds, all of a savage nature." Her niece, Catharine Holley, was with Sebastian in Cabeza de Lobo and witnessed his terrible death. When she returned to New Orleans, she told the story to Violet, who refused to believe her. To prevent others from hearing it, she has committed Catharine to a mental institution. Now Violet invites an ambitious young neurosurgeon, Dr. Cukrowicz, to examine Catharine, hoping that he will perform an experimental surgical procedure on her (a lobotomy) to silence her once and for all. In return, she will make a sizable donation to his hospital. If he refuses, she'll withhold her money, making it difficult for him to continue his experimental work. Catharine's mother and brother also pressure Catharine to stop telling the terrible story of Sebastian's death, for fear that if she won't, Violet will cut them out of his will, leaving them destitute.

Catharine wants to tell the truth about what she's seen, but it's in no one else's interest that she do so. In this world, everyone but Catharine uses others for their own ends. This, Williams says, is how the world works. Violet used Sebastian to make her feel important as they traveled the world together; Sebastian used his mother to help attract boys to him. Then he used Catharine the same way when she became his traveling companion, after Violet was incapacitated by a stroke. Family members use each other; the rich use the needy; scientists violate their principles to get ahead; all of us devour each other. Williams gives to Catharine the line that sums up this relationship: "Yes, we all use each other and that's what we think of as love, and not being able to use each other is what's — *hate*. . . ."

After Catharine tells the story, not only of Sebastian's death but of his life of using others for his own pleasure, Dr. Cukrowicz is uncertain. "I think we ought to at least consider the possibility that the girl's story could be true. . . ." he says. What will he do? Will he succumb to Violet's offer of money and perform the lobotomy that would deprive Catharine of both her freedom and her personality, or will he refuse? In an early draft of the play, Cukrowicz believes her and refuses to operate. In the final version, Williams, truer to his pessimistic outlook, leaves us in suspense.

In one of his last plays, *Something Cloudy, Something Clear*, Williams seems to reconcile himself to this give-and-take as an inescapable part of existence, and forgives his characters for doing what is only human. In this play, people use each other for everything from professional advantage to sex to safety and shelter. There is nothing to be done about it, Williams now seems to say, but to accept it as an inescapable risk if one is going to have relationships with others. It is hope that brings people together, after all, and there is always the chance that, as in *The Rose Tattoo*, the result will be love. When, at the end of that play, Serafina cries out, feeling a child growing in her body, she is referring not only to the life within her, but to her life and Alvaro's, joined against all odds: "Two, two lives again, two!"

GAY THEMES

In 1960, when it was still impermissible to write about gay characters in plays and even novels without condemning them, Williams wrote, "I dare to suggest . . . that the theatre has made in our time its greatest artistic advance through the unlocking and lighting up and ventilation of the closets, attics, and basements of human behavior and experience."

Every person's journey toward sexual understanding is different. For a gay person born in the early years of the twentieth century and who came of age in its middle years, it could be especially difficult. Sexual matters in general were not talked of. When they were, the images and models available to most young people were of heterosexual sex — not only in daily life (including all means of advertising) but in literature, films, and the theater. When homosexuality was talked of at all, it was usually in derogatory terms. Homosexuals were considered to be willfully perverted, or at best, mentally ill people who might be cured, but only if they wanted to be. When they were portrayed, they were sinister villains out to "convert" innocent young heterosexuals, or sad, guilt-ridden alcoholics whose tragic lives ended in suicide. The men were sissies who liked classical music and embroidery; the women were "mannish." A "happy ending" for these characters — and for the audience — consisted of discovering that they weren't gay after all.

Between 1927 and 1968, it was illegal to produce plays in New York that displayed "sex perversion," which was always taken to mean homosexuals. If a producer was found guilty of presenting such a play he was subject to a large fine and the theater where the play was presented would be padlocked for a year, depriving its owner of significant income. Authorities were reluctant to apply the law due to the vagueness of its language, so only a few plays with gay or lesbian characters were shut down, while many (including plays by Tennessee Williams) were produced. Still, the existence of the law and the fact that it occasionally was enforced indicate the cultural climate regarding homosexuality at the time when Williams wrote most of his plays.

This was the world and the theater in which Williams grew up. When he finally became fully aware of his homosexuality, in 1939, he wasted little time including gay characters in his work. Indeed, a year earlier, he had included one, a gay prisoner named The Queen, in *Not About Nightingales*. The second, a tormented young man named Eloi, appears in a one-act most likely written in 1941, called *Auto-Da-Fé*. The gay characters that Williams created after Eloi would not be tormented by the fact of their homosexuality, as some critics have claimed. While they might have some homophobic, self-hating thoughts (and some do), the important point is that they struggle against them. They may have guilt about sex in general, but not about being gay. Because Williams, who was a person of his times, found coming out to be difficult and because the depiction of gay characters carried such a heavy professional risk, he developed a strategy (probably not a conscious one) of revealing something of his gay characters' sexuality while concealing other things. This need to reveal versus an urge to conceal was another ongoing theme in Williams' work that expressed itself as a dichotomy.

Williams wrote more explicitly about sex as a motivating, powerful force than any American playwright before him. This alone made him controversial. Writing about gay characters made his work even more distasteful to some critics, who routinely called those characters "queers" and "perverts." This did not deter Williams. In 1953, when the federal government was hunting not only for communists but for homosexuals within its ranks, and Broadway was producing plays that included gay characters who were ridiculed because they were different, killed themselves, or promised never to be gay again, Williams wrote *Camino Real*.

One of the play's characters, borrowed from Marcel Proust's *A la recherché du temps perdu*, is the Baron de Charlus. The Baron is not only gay, but is very out and actively cruising for sex, until he is killed by agents of the government. In this play, Williams does not ask for the audience's tolerance or understanding; he simply includes a gay person — and an outlandish figure, at that — as a fact of life. The Baron's fate at the hand of society was another fact. (The play opened a month after President Eisenhower signed Executive Order #10450, which instructed heads of departments and all those who did hiring that "sexual perversion" was not only sufficient but necessary grounds for disqualification from federal jobs, and this order was soon adopted by many state and local governments.)

In *Cat on a Hot Tin Roof*, Williams used a familiar archetype — the all-American football hero — to illustrate the moral paralysis that can overcome an otherwise honest person when he tries to deny a crucial part of his identity (in this case his sexuality) in order to retain his position not only within his own family but also in society. The play asks, how does one tell the truth amid the lies that families and societies tell each other about a whole host of subjects? *Suddenly Last Summer* is in part the story of a man who lives his life at the very edge of sexual boundaries without apology and is willing to pay the price.

In the 1970s, with the arrival of the modern gay liberation movement, it became somewhat more permissible to write with honesty and without judgment about gay characters in theater and literature. For Williams, who had been writing about gay characters in his plays and stories for forty years, this was a chance to be more explicit than he often had been about their sexual histories. Now, however, whereas critics of the 1950s accused Williams of being "too gay," gay activists charged that he was not being gay enough. They demanded that

Williams — and other writers — create only "positive images" of gay people. It was never Williams' intent to write "positive images" of any sort of person. Those who criticize Williams on this point avoid commenting on the "negative images" of straight people in his plays, including those who murder, betray, or leave others in need. Nonetheless, this was not an argument that Williams could win. Like any writer, he could only write as he needed to write, regardless of what critics — especially those driven by political agendas — would say.

LATER DEVELOPMENTS

By 1962, Williams had been a public figure for over twenty years. Audiences had acquired fixed expectations of his work, and they recognized and came to expect a thematic pattern, even as it varied from play to play and in some plays didn't appear at all: An itinerant figure who embodies a life force, often exemplified as a sexual one, enters a closed, tradition-bound community. He finds a companion whose spiritual aspirations and physical desires have been crushed by that community, which values conformity above all. The stranger reawakens the life force in this companion and in doing so arouses fierce opposition in the community, which responds with brutal retaliation in the form of punishment and often death to either the stranger or his companion or both. In the ensuing struggle, individual expression, including sexual and spiritual expression, is highly valued. If either or both of the two principal characters die, a tragedy has occurred. This pattern, in many variations of a struggle between physical or spiritual vitality and death, can be seen in, among other plays, *Battle of Angels*, *Summer and Smoke*, *A Streetcar Named Desire*, *The Rose Tattoo*, *Camino Real*, *Cat on a Hot Tin Roof*, and *The Night of the Iguana*.

Beginning with *The Milk Train Doesn't Stop Here Anymore*, this pattern changed. Reversals in Williams' career and personal life account in part for this transformation. By the early 1960s, Williams was one of the three leading playwrights in America, alongside Arthur Miller and William Inge. No matter how much success he attained, however, and no matter how widely and obsessively he traveled, he could not outrun "the enemy inside" him, the "blue devil" that had been accompanying him since he was a young man. Beginning in the mid-1950s, while working on *Cat on a Hot Tin Roof*, his drinking increased, and he was taking stimulants such as Benzedrine as well as depressives like barbiturates. In 1948 he had met an ex-Marine named Frank Merlo in Provincetown, Massachusetts, and they soon became partners. Merlo became the foundation of Williams' daily life, organizing all the details that Williams was unable to handle. By the late 1950s, their relationship was fraying. By 1961, it was damaged beyond repair, and in 1963, Merlo died of lung cancer.

Merlo's death plunged Williams into despair and a depression that lasted the rest of the decade. His intake of alcohol and drugs increased dramatically; he began relying on a series of companions to look after him, not all of whom had his best interests at heart. This downward spiral reached its nadir in September 1969, when Dakin Williams, alarmed at his brother's physical and mental condition, convinced him to admit himself to the psychiatric ward at Barnes Hospital in St. Louis. He was there for three months recovering (not completely, it turned out) from his addictions and regaining his mental stability. His worst nightmare had come true, however; he had been confined in close quarters for the longest period in his life. Although Dakin's actions saved his life, he never forgave his brother.

When he was released in December, Williams returned to his home in Key West and resumed writing. However, the years of depression and drugs, along with a paranoia that had become a major personality trait, had its effect on his work.

For all of his troubles during these years, however, Williams was quite aware of the tremendous dramaturgical changes the theater had undergone in the two decades since he had written *The Glass Menagerie*, and his own work began to reflect them. The barbarism of World War

II and the fears of the Cold War had caused artists to find methods of depicting a world in which the Holocaust was possible and where the threat of atomic destruction was ever present. The result was that many dramaturgical conventions that had been taken as normal and natural for a century were destabilized. Linear narratives, three-dimensional characters and their central place in a theatrical event, action that gave meaning to the lives of characters and audiences alike, all were being questioned and often replaced with experiments in form and expression that playwrights believed better reflected life in a world threatened by nuclear destruction.

Conflict, the basis of drama in the West since Aristotle's *Poetics*, was replaced, by Samuel Beckett, with stasis. Stable identity was fragmented by Harold Pinter, so that a character might seem to be a different person, with a different history, each time he entered the room. Exposition, the presumption of an agreed-upon past, was banished altogether. The notion that a character's actions had a significant meaning (and that our own lives had significant meaning that could be located in a force or being outside ourselves) was replaced by writers like Jean Genet with a world where people were little more than the sum of their various disguises. All of these trends had roots in late- nineteenth- and early-twentieth-century writers such as Maurice Maeterlinck, August Strindberg, and Luigi Pirandello; now they became the practice of playwrights worldwide.

Williams was aware of all these developments. He was deeply impressed by the work of Beckett, Genet, Pinter, and the young Edward Albee, and he adopted many of their techniques as a way of expressing his own current view of the world. He was intrigued enough by Samuel Beckett to invest in the first American production of *Waiting for Godot*, in 1956. In 1957, he met the Japanese writer Yukio Mishima, having been impressed with his *Five Modern No Plays*. On a trip to Japan, he saw No and Kabuki plays and was attracted to their calm atmosphere, their ritual, and to No's emphasis on transcendence. Williams experimented with No techniques first in *The*

Day on Which a Man Dies, written about 1958, and then in *The Milk Train Doesn't Stop Here Anymore* and *In the Bar of a Tokyo Hotel*.

In his late works, characters who fight for life and dignity still retain some stature, but they are also apt to be grotesque, outsized comic figures who refuse to give up the struggle and accept the peace that death offers. *Milk Train*'s Flora Goforth, who has cancer but refuses to die, is an example. So is the title character in *The Gnädiges Fraulein*, a former entertainer who now must fight giant cocaloony birds for fish in order to earn her keep in a boarding house in the Florida Keys. There are many more. In plays like *The Gnädiges Fraulein*, *Now the Cats with Jewelled Claws*, *The Mutilated*, *The Remarkable Rooming-House of Mme. Lemonde*, and *Kirche, Kutchen und Kinder*, the characters are no longer three-dimensional human beings. Instead, they are cartoons in an outrageous, cartoonish world whose lives suggest that struggle is either sad or absurd.

Sex, once the life-giving force that had saved so many of Williams' characters, also becomes grotesque. In *Milk Train*, Christopher Flanders stumbles into the play having been attacked by dogs, his clothes nearly torn off of him. He is a descendant of Val Xavier and Stanley Kowalski, but here he is, at first, something of a figure of fun. Soon, we realize that not only is he no life force, but is, in fact, the Angel of Death, come to help ease Flora out of this world. Sex, once a life force for Williams, here is associated with death.

Lyrical language, once Williams' stock in trade, is now fragmented. Long speeches that were rich in imagery and moved on waves of powerful rhythms are broken up and reduced to a few words. In the extremity of their pain and confusion, characters have difficulty completing a sentence. Compare this brief exchange between two characters, called One and Two, from *I Can't Imagine Tomorrow*, written about 1966, with Blanche's speech from *Streetcar*, quoted previously. "One" is a woman who rarely leaves the house; "Two" is her only friend, a man so paralyzed by fear that he hasn't taught his high school class for five days:

Two: Today. Today I did go.

One: To the clinic?

Two: Yes. There.

One: What did you tell them? What did they tell you?

Two: I only talked to the girl, the —

One: Receptionist?

Two: Yes, she gave me a paper, a —

One: An application, a —

Two: Questionnaire, to —

One: Fill out?

Two: I — I had to inform them if I —

One: Yes?

Two: Had ever had —

One: Psychiatric?

Two: Treatment, or been — hospitalized.

The common condition of many of Williams' characters after 1962 is one of tremendous existential pain and the inability to overcome it. Williams did not, however, fully desert all of his former values or dramatic procedures. In plays such as *Small Craft Warnings*, *Vieux Carré*, *A Lovely Sunday for Creve Coeur*, and *Something Cloudy, Something Clear*, he returned to more fully drawn characters who reach for eloquence in a recognizable world. In these plays, Williams' debt to Chekhov resurfaces, as characters search for love and peace, and are granted by their author forgiveness and understanding.

Critics and audiences were, for the most part, baffled and even angered by Williams' late plays. He had moved far from the kind of play they expected of him, plays such as *The Glass Menagerie* and *A Streetcar Named Desire*, which, even as they broke new ground in language, design, or subject matter, were within traditions that audiences recognized. It did not help Williams' cause that many of his later works were produced on Broadway, which attracts the most conservative audiences and critics and where the large theaters, with their high proscenium arches and stages separated from the audience by orchestra pits, were unsuited for the styles Williams was exploring.

Williams was painfully aware of responses of this sort and was angered that critics judged his new plays by old criteria. In *The Politics of Reputation: The Critical Reception of Tennessee Williams' Later Plays*, Annette J. Saddik observes:

> During the 1960s Williams claimed that he was deliberately moving away from what the critical establishment saw as the essentially realistic dramatic forms that had established his career to what Lillian Hellman called "the theater of the imagination" — a more antirealistic, fragmented type of drama characteristic of the new movements of the time. He insisted that the negative critical reception of this later work was a result of the critics' failure to set aside their "fixed image" of him as a realistic playwright and evaluate the later plays on their own terms. . .[T]he deliberate changes from his early work to the later work in terms of style and presentation were disturbing to the majority of critics, and . . . their nostalgia for a play such as *The Glass Menagerie* was preventing them from understanding and/or accepting his later experiments with language and dramatic form.

The critical reception his later plays received, whether harsh or indifferent, did not deter Williams from writing. Indeed, he was as prolific in his last years as he had been during the height of his fame. Each morning he rose early, made a pot of strong black coffee, and worked for several hours on the portable typewriter that, like the volume of poems by Hart Crane, accompanied him on his seemingly endless travels. Still, and although his older plays were being continuously revived with great success, the failure of his new plays, and loneliness, weighed on him. At the end of November 1981, after completing the first draft of a new play called *The Lingering Hour*, he wrote, "I have been through much illness of the body: the end of my life cannot be predicted with any precision but I'm aware that it will come soon enough. I am tired."

Lyle Leverich writes that in the last month of his life, Williams seemed to sense that the end was near. He closed his house in New Orleans and said to his housekeeper of more than thirty years, Leoncia McGee, "Lee, I don't know if I'll ever see you again." He made plans to sell his house in New Orleans. He traveled — alone, for the first time in decades — to London, Rome, and Taormina, Sicily, before returning to New York in February 1983. The few friends who saw him in this period were shocked by his apparent exhaustion and lack of spirit. He took a suite in the Elysée Hotel, and asked his friend John Uecker to stay with him. He saw few people and ate little. On the night of February 24, Williams, Uecker, and his friend Jane Smith, whom he had known for more than forty years, had dinner and then watched television in his suite. Williams was, Uecker told Smith, in better spirits than he'd been for months.

The next morning, Uecker discovered Williams' body crouched beside his bed. He had been drinking and had taken enough barbiturates to cause an overdose. The cap from a prescription bottle had gotten lodged in his throat, and Williams, the medical examiner later said, died of asphyxiation.

For many years Williams had said that he wanted to be buried at sea, his body dropped overboard near the spot where Hart Crane had thrown himself into the Gulf of Mexico. Instead, Dakin Williams decided that his brother would be buried in the family plot in Calvary Cemetery in St. Louis, an accessible place where a writer of his stature deserved to lay. He was buried there on March 5.

In recent years critics have become more interested in the post-*Iguana* plays and have begun to appreciate their roots in other kinds of theater and their experimentalism. Still, opinion on Williams' late plays remains divided. Keith Hack, who directed the successful British production of *Vieux Carré* at the Nottingham Playhouse in

1978 and in London, said in an interview in *Studies in American Drama, 1945–Present*:

> Tennessee felt a need in the 60's to be, as he had been in the 40's and 50's, in the dangerous 'avant garde.' The sixties was very youth oriented; there were a lot of new, young writers. It was great to be young and it wasn't great to be fifty; it was an automatic disqualification. And I think Tennessee tried to write a number of overtly experimental plays not, I think, in the mainstream of his writing — some of it very beautiful because he was a great poet, but in terms of theatre technique and character work appeared like a self-conscious attempt to be relevant and *au courant*.

On the other hand, Philip C. Kolin defends the later plays as wide-ranging experiments in both form and substance. In *The Undiscovered Country: The Later Plays of Tennessee Williams*, he writes:

> Labels, however, have concealed Williams accomplishments in his later plays. The diversity and breadth of this part of the Williams canon defies easy, homogenized rubrics. Not even the convoluted classification system of Polonious — "pastoral, comical, historical pastoral, tragical-historical, tragical-comical-historical-pastoral — can do justice to the highly experimental plays of Williams's last three decades.

Kolin then describes Williams' late plays as "triumphs of the American theatre in the 1960s, 1970s and 1980s."

Producers, however, aware that many audiences tend to favor plays they know over those that are new to them, have been slow to put these later works to the test. Until the late plays become more frequently produced, we won't know if new audiences will find them to be unsuccessful attempts at being modish, or ways of seeing the world in terms that are as ahead of their time as *The Glass Menagerie* and *A Streetcar Named Desire*.

DRAMATIC MOMENTS

from the Major Plays

These short excerpts are from the playwright's major plays. They give a taste of the work of the playwright. Each has a short introduction in brackets that helps the reader understand the context of the excerpt. The excerpts, which are in chronological order, illustrate the main themes mentioned in the In an Hour essay. Premiere date is given.

from **THE GLASS MENAGERIE** (1944)

from Scene Four

CHARACTERS

Tom
Laura
Amanda

[Tom and his sister, Laura, live with their mother, Amanda, in a cramped apartment in St. Louis during the Depression. Their father left the family many years before. Tom supports the family by working as a clerk in a shoe warehouse; at night he writes poetry and dreams of escaping his dreary existence. Laura lives in a world of her own imagination, having withdrawn from the one around her due to sensitivity to her limp. Despite her mother's attempts to find her a job, she spends most of her time at home, polishing small glass figurines she keeps in a cabinet. Amanda works hard to see that Laura will be able to cope with the world, either by becoming self-sufficient or finding a husband, and enlists Tom in an attempt at the latter.]

(Immediately following, the church bell is heard striking six. At the sixth stroke the alarm goes off in Amanda's room, and after a few moments we hear her calling: "Rise and Shine! Rise and Shine! Laura, go tell your brother to rise and shine!")

TOM: *(Sitting up slowly.)* I'll rise — but I won't shine.

(The light increases.)

AMANDA: Laura, tell your brother his coffee is ready.

(Laura slips into the front room.)

LAURA: Tom! — It's nearly seven. Don't make mother nervous.

(He stares stupidly.)

LAURA: (*Beseechingly.*) Tom, speak to mother this morning. Make up with her, apologize, speak to her!

TOM: She won't to me. It's her that started not speaking.

LAURA: If you just say you're sorry she'll start speaking.

TOM: Her not speaking — is that such a tragedy?

LAURA: Please — please!

AMANDA: (*Calling from the kitchenette.*) Laura, are you going to do what I asked you to do, or do I have to get dressed and go out myself?

LAURA: Going, going — soon as I get on my coat!

(She pulls on a shapeless felt hat with a nervous, jerky movement, pleadingly glancing at Tom. She rushes awkwardly for her coat. The coat is one of Amanda's, inaccurately made-over, the sleeves too short for Laura.)

Butter and what else?

AMANDA: (*Entering from the kitchenette.*) Just butter. Tell them to charge it.

LAURA: Mother, they make such faces when I do that.

AMANDA: Sticks and stones can break our bones, but the expression on Mr. Garfinkle's face won't harm us! Tell your brother his coffee is getting cold.

LAURA: (*At the door.*) Do what I asked you, will you, Tom?

(He looks sullenly away.)

AMANDA: Laura, go now or just don't go at all!

LAURA: (*Rushing out.*) Going — going!

(A second later she cries out. Tom springs up and crosses to the door. Tom opens the door.)

TOM: Laura?

LAURA: I'm all right. I slipped, but I'm all right.

AMANDA: (*Peering anxiously after her.*) If anyone breaks a leg on those fire-escape steps, the landlord ought to be sued for every cent he possesses! (*She shuts the door. Now she remembers she isn't speaking to Tom and returns to the other room.*)

(As Tom comes listlessly for his coffee, she turns her back to him and stands rigidly facing the window on the gloomy gray vault of the areaway. Its light on her face with its aged but childish features is cruelly sharp, satirical as a Daumier print.)

(The music of "Ave Maria" is heard softly.)

(Tom glances sheepishly but sullenly at her averted figure and slumps at the table. The coffee is scalding hot; he sips it and gasps and spits it back in the cup. At his gasp, Amanda catches her breath and half turns. Then she catches herself and turns back to the window. Tom blows on his coffee, glancing sidewise at his mother. She clears her throat. Tom clears his. He starts to rise, sinks back down again, scratches his head, clears his throat again. Amanda coughs. Tom raises his cup in both hands to blow on it, his eyes staring over the rim of it at his mother for several moments. Then he slowly sets the cup down and awkwardly and hesitantly rises from the chair.)

TOM: (*Hoarsely.*) Mother. I — I apologize, Mother.

(Amanda draws a quick, shuddering breath. Her face works grotesquely. She breaks into childlike tears.)

I'm sorry for what I said, for everything that I said, I didn't mean it.

AMANDA: (*Sobbingly.*) My devotion has made me a witch and so I make myself hateful to my children!

TOM: *No*, you *don't.*

AMANDA: I worry so much, don't sleep, it makes me nervous!

TOM: (*Gently.*) I understand that.

AMANDA: I've had to put up a solitary battle all these years. But you're my right-hand bower! Don't fall down, don't fail!

TOM: (*Gently.*) I try, Mother.

AMANDA: (*With great enthusiasm.*) Try and you will *succeed!* (*The notion makes her breathless.*) Why, you — you're just *full* of natural endowments! Both of my children — they're *unusual* children! Don't you

think I know it? I'm so — *proud!* Happy and — feel I've — so much
to be thankful for but — promise me one thing, son!

TOM: What, Mother?

AMANDA: Promise, son, you'll — never be a drunkard!

TOM: (*Turns to her grinning.*) I will never be a drunkard, Mother.

AMANDA: That's what frightened me so, that you'd be drinking! Eat a
bowl of Purina!

TOM: Just coffee, Mother.

AMANDA: Shredded wheat biscuit?

TOM: No. No, Mother, just coffee.

AMANDA: You can't put in a day's work on an empty stomach. You've
got ten minutes — don't gulp! Drinking too-hot liquids makes cancer of the stomach . . . Put cream in.

TOM: No, thank you.

AMANDA: To cool it.

TOM: No! No, thank you, I want it black.

AMANDA: I know, but it's not good for you. We have to do all that we
can to build ourselves up. In these trying times we live in, all that
we have to cling to is — each other. . . . That's why it's so important
to — Tom — I — I sent out your sister so I could discuss something
with you. If you hadn't spoken I would have spoken to you. (*She
sits down.*)

TOM: (*Gently.*) What is it, Mother, that you want to discuss?

AMANDA: *Laura!*

(*Tom puts his cup down slowly.*)
(*Legend on screen: "Laura." Music: "The Glass Menagerie.")*

TOM: — Oh. — Laura . . .

AMANDA: (*Touching his sleeve.*) You know how Laura is. So quiet — but
still waters run deep! She notices things and I think she — broods
about them.

(*Tom looks up.*)

A few days ago when I came in she was crying.

TOM: What about?

AMANDA: You.

TOM: Me?

AMANDA: She has an idea that you're not happy here.

TOM: What gave her that idea?

AMANDA: What gives her any idea? However, you do act strangely. I
— I'm not criticizing, understand *that!* I know your ambitions do
not lie in the warehouse, that like everybody in the whole wide
world — you've had to — make sacrifices, but — Tom — Tom —
life's not easy, it calls for — Spartan endurance! There's so many
things in my heart that I cannot describe to you! I've never told you
but I — *loved* your father. . . .

TOM: (*Gently.*) I know that, Mother.

AMANDA: And you — when I see you taking after his ways! Staying
out late — and — well, you *had* been drinking the night you were
in that — terrifying condition! Laura says that you hate the apartment and that you go out nights to get away from it! Is that true,
Tom?

TOM: No. You say there's so much in your heart that you can't describe
to me. That's true of me, too. There's so much in my heart that I
can't describe to *you!* So let's respect each other's —

AMANDA: But why — *why,* Tom — are you always so *restless?* Where
do you go to, nights?

TOM: I — go to the movies.

AMANDA: Why do you go to the movies so much, Tom?

TOM: I go to the movies because — I like adventure. Adventure is something I don't have much of at work, so I go to the movies.

AMANDA: But, Tom, you go to the movies *entirely* too *much!*

TOM: I like a lot of adventure.

(*Amanda looks baffled, then hurt. As the familiar inquisition resumes,
Tom becomes hard and impatient again. Amanda slips back into her queru-
lous attitude toward him.*)

(Image on screen: A sailing vessel with Jolly Roger.)

AMANDA: Most young men find adventure in their careers.

TOM: Then most young men are not employed in a warehouse.

AMANDA: The world is full of young men employed in warehouses and offices and factories.

TOM: Do all of them find adventure in their careers?

AMANDA: They do or they do without it! Not everybody has a craze for adventure.

TOM: Man is by instinct a lover, a hunter, a fighter, and none of these instincts are given much play at the warehouse!

AMANDA: Man is by instinct! Don't quote instinct to me! Instinct is something that people have got away from! It belongs to animals! Christian adults don't want it!

TOM: What do Christian adults want, then, Mother?

AMANDA: Superior things! Things of the mind and the spirit! Only animals have to satisfy instincts! Surely your aims are somewhat higher than theirs! Than monkeys — pigs —

TOM: I reckon they're not.

AMANDA: You're joking. However, that isn't what I wanted to discuss.

TOM: (*Rising.*) I haven't much time.

AMANDA: (*Pushing his shoulder.*) Sit down.

TOM: You want me to punch in red at the warehouse, Mother?

AMANDA: You have five minutes. I want to talk about Laura. (*Screen legend: "Plans and Provisions."*)

TOM: All right! What about Laura?

AMANDA: We have to be making some plans and provisions for her. She's older than you, two years, and nothing has happened. She just drifts along doing nothing. It frightens me terribly how she just drifts along.

TOM: I guess she's the type that people call home girls.

AMANDA: There's no such type, and if there is, it's a pity! That is unless the home is hers, with a husband!

TOM: What?

AMANDA: Oh, I can see the handwriting on the wall as plain as I see the nose on my face! It's terrifying! More and more you remind me of your father! He was out all hours without explanation! — Then *left!* *Good-bye!* And me with the bag to hold. I saw that letter you got from the Merchant Marine. I know what you're dreaming of. I'm not standing here blindfolded. (*She pauses.*) Very well, then. Then *do* it! But not till there's somebody to take your place.

****

from **A STREETCAR NAMED DESIRE** (1947)
from Scene Two

CHARACTERS

> Blanche
> Stella
> Stanley
> Steve
> Pablo

[Blanche Dubois, a young widow, comes to visit her sister Stella and Stella's husband, Stanley, in their apartment in the French Quarter of New Orleans shortly after the end of World War II. Stanley quickly dislikes and distrusts Blanche, whom he finds affected. He suspects her of robbing Stella of their family home, Belle Reve, which Blanche claims was lost in bankruptcy proceedings. He confronts her as she enters the bathroom after taking a bath.]

> *(It is six o'clock the following evening. Blanche is bathing. Stella is completing her toilette. Blanche's dress, a flowered print, is laid out on Stella's bed.*
>
> > *Stanley enters the kitchen from outside, leaving the door open on the perpetual "blue piano" around the corner.)*
>
> *(Stella goes out to the porch. Blanche comes out of the bathroom in a red satin robe.)*

BLANCHE: (*Airily.*) Hello, Stanley! Here I am, all freshly bathed and scented, and feeling like a brand new human being!

> *(He lights a cigarette.)*

STANLEY: That's good.

BLANCHE: (*Drawing the curtains at the window.*) Excuse me while I slip on my pretty new dress!

STANLEY: Go right ahead, Blanche.

(*She closes the drapes between the rooms.*)

BLANCHE: I understand there's to be a little card party to which we ladies are cordially *not* invited!

STANLEY: (*Ominously.*) Yeah?

(*Blanche throws off her robe and slips into a flowered print dress.*)

BLANCHE: Where's Stella?

STANLEY: Out on the porch.

BLANCHE: I'm going to ask a favor of you in a moment.

STANLEY: What could that be, I wonder?

BLANCHE: Some buttons in back! You may enter!

(*He crosses through drapes with a smoldering look.*)

BLANCHE: How do I look?

STANLEY: You look all right.

BLANCHE: Many thanks! Now the buttons!

STANLEY: I can't do nothing with them.

BLANCHE: You men with your big clumsy fingers. May I have a drag on your cig?

STANLEY: Have one for yourself.

BLANCHE: Why, thanks! . . . It looks like my trunk has exploded.

STANLEY: Me an' Stella were helping you unpack.

BLANCHE: Well, you certainly did a fast and thorough job of it!

STANLEY: It looks like you raided some stylish shops in Paris.

BLANCHE: Ha-ha! Yes — clothes are my passion!

STANLEY: What does it cost for a string of fur-pieces like that?

BLANCHE: Why, those were a tribute from an admirer of mine!

STANLEY: He must have had a lot of — admiration!

BLANCHE: Oh, in my youth I excited some admiration. But look at me now! (*She smiles at him radiantly.*) Would you think it possible that I was once considered to be — attractive?

STANLEY: Your looks are OK.

BLANCHE: I was fishing for a compliment, Stanley.

STANLEY: I don't go in for that stuff.

BLANCHE: What — stuff?

STANLEY: Compliments to women about their looks. I never met a woman that didn't know if she was good-looking or not without being told, and some of them give themselves credit for more than they've got. I once went out with a doll who said to me, "I am the glamorous type, I am the glamorous type!" I said, "So what?"

BLANCHE: And what did she say then?

STANLEY: She didn't say nothing. That shut her up like a clam.

BLANCHE: Did it end the romance?

STANLEY: It ended the conversation — that was all. Some men are took in by this Hollywood glamour stuff and some men are not.

BLANCHE: I'm sure you belong in the second category.

STANLEY: That's right.

BLANCHE: I cannot imagine any witch of a woman casting a spell over you.

STANLEY: That's — right.

BLANCHE: You're simple, straightforward and honest, a little bit on the primitive side I should think. To interest you a woman would have to — (*She pauses with an indefinite gesture.*)

STANLEY: (*Slowly.*) Lay . . . her cards on the table.

BLANCHE: (*Smiling.*) Well, I never cared for wishy-washy people. That's why, when you walked in here last night, I said to myself — "My sister has married a man!" — Of course that was all I could tell about you.

STANLEY: (*Booming.*) Now let's cut the re-bop!

BLANCHE: (*Pressing her hands to her ears.*) Ouuuuu!

STELLA: (*Calling from the steps.*) Stanley! You come out here and let Blanche finishing dressing!

BLANCHE: I'm through dressing, honey.

STELLA: Well, you come out, then.

STANLEY: Your sister and I are having a little talk.

BLANCHE: (*Lightly.*) Honey, do me a favor. Run to the drugstore and get me a lemon Coke with plenty of chipped ice in it! — Will you do that for me, sweetie?

STELLA: (*Uncertainly.*) Yes. (*She goes around the corner of the building.*)

BLANCHE: The poor thing was out there listening to us, and I have an idea she doesn't understand you as well as I do . . . . All right; now, Mr. Kowalski, let's proceed without any more double-talk. I'm ready to answer all questions. I've nothing to hide. What is it?

STANLEY: There is such a thing in the state of Louisiana as the Napoleonic code, according to which whatever belongs to my wife is also mine — and vice versa.

BLANCHE: My, but you have an impressive judicial air! (*She sprays herself with her atomizer; then playfully sprays him with it. He seizes the atomizer and slams it down on the dresser. She throws back her head and laughs.*)

STANLEY: If I didn't know that you was my wife's sister I'd get ideas about you!

BLANCHE: Such as what?

STANLEY: Don't play so dumb. You know what!

BLANCHE: (*She puts the atomizer on the table.*) All right. Cards on the table. That suits me. (*She turns toward Stanley.*) I know I fib a good deal. After all, a woman's charm is fifty per cent illusion, but when a thing is important I tell the truth, and this is the truth: I haven't cheated my sister or you or anyone else as long as I have lived.

STANLEY: Where's the papers? In the trunk?

(*Stanley crosses to the trunk, shoves it roughly open and begins to open compartments.*)

BLANCHE: What in the name of heaven are you thinking of! What's in the back of that little boy's mind of yours? That I am absconding

with something, attempting some kind of treachery on my sister? —
Let me do that! It will be faster and simpler . . . (*She crosses to the
trunk and takes out a box.*) I keep my papers mostly in this tin box.
(*She opens it.*)

STANLEY: What's them underneath? (*He indicates another sheaf of paper.*)

BLANCHE: Those are love-letters, yellowing with antiquity, all from
one boy.

(*He snatches them up. She speaks fiercely.*)

BLANCHE: Give those back to me!

STANLEY: I'll have a look at them first!

BLANCHE: The touch of your hands insults them!

STANLEY: Don't pull that stuff!

(*He rips off the ribbon and starts to examine them. Blanche snatches them
from him, and they cascade to the floor.*)

BLANCHE: Now that you've touched them I'll burn them!

STANLEY: (*Staring, baffled.*) What in hell are they?

BLANCHE: (*On the floor gathering them up.*) Poems a dead boy wrote. I
hurt him the way that you would like to hurt me, but you can't! I'm
not young and vulnerable any more. But my young husband was
and I — never mind about that! Just give them back to me!

STANLEY: What do you mean by saying you'll have to burn them?

BLANCHE: I'm sorry, I must have lost my head for a moment. Everyone has something he won't let others touch because of their —
intimate nature . . . (*She now seems faint with exhaustion and she sits
down with the strong box and puts on a pair of glasses and goes methodi-
cally through a large stack of papers.*) Ambler & Ambler. Hmmmmm
. . . Crabtree . . . More Ambler & Ambler.

STANLEY: What is Ambler & Ambler?

BLANCHE: A firm that made loans on the place.

STANLEY: Then it *was* lost on a mortgage?

BLANCHE (*Touching her forehead.*) That must've been what happened.

STANLEY: I don't want no ifs, ands or buts! What's all the rest of them papers?

(*She hands him the entire box. He carries it to the table and starts to examine the papers.*)

BLANCHE: (*Picking up a large envelope containing more papers.*) There are thousands of papers, stretching back over hundreds of years, affecting Belle Reve as, piece by piece, our improvident grandfathers and father and uncles and brothers exchanged the land for their epic fornications — to put it plainly! (*She removes her glasses with an exhausted laugh.*) The four-letter word deprived us of our plantation, till finally all that was left — and Stella can verify that! — was the house itself and about twenty acres of ground, including a graveyard, to which now all but Stella and I have retreated. (*She pours all the contents of the envelope on the table.*) Here all of them are, all papers! I hereby endow you with them! Take them, peruse them — commit them to memory, even! I think it's wonderfully fitting that Belle Reve should finally be this bunch of old papers in your big, capable hands! . . . I wonder if Stella's coming back with my lemon Coke . . . (*She leans back and closes her eyes.*)

STANLEY: I have a lawyer acquaintance who will study this case out.

BLANCHE: Present them to him with a box of aspirin tablets.

STANLEY: (*Becoming somewhat sheepish.*) You see, under the Napoleonic code — a man has to take an interest in his wife's affairs — especially now that she's going to have a baby.

(*Blanche opens her eyes. The "blue piano" sounds louder.*)

BLANCHE: Stella? Stella going to have a baby? (*Dreamily.*) I didn't know she was going to have a baby!

(*She gets up and crosses to the outside door. Stella appears around the corner with a carton from the drugstore.*)
(*Stanley goes into the bedroom with the envelope and the box.*)

(The inner rooms fade to darkness and the outside wall of the house is visible. Blanche meets Stella at the foot of the steps to the sidewalk.)

BLANCHE: Stella, Stella for star! How lovely to have a baby! It's all right! Everything's all right.

STELLA: I'm sorry he did that to you.

BLANCHE: Oh, I guess he's just not the type that goes for jasmine perfume, but maybe he's what we need to mix with our blood now that we've lost Belle Reve. We thrashed it out. I feel a bit shaky, but I think I handled it nicely, I laughed and treated it all as a joke. *(Steve and Pablo appear, carrying a case of beer.)* I called him a little boy and laughed and flirted. Yes, I was flirting with your husband! *(As the men approach.)* The guests are gathering for the poker party. *(The two men pass between them, and enter the house.)* Which way do we go now, Stella — this way?

STELLA: No, this way. *(She leads Blanche away.)*

BLANCHE: *(Laughing.)* The blind are leading the blind!

(A tamale Vendor is heard calling.)

VENDOR'S VOICE: Red-hot!

****

from **CAMINO REAL** (1953)

(pronounced *Camino Real*)

from Block Three

CHARACTERS

Kilroy
Officer
Street People
Rosita
Nursie
Gypsy
Gypsy's Loudspeaker
Loudspeaker
Abdullah
Bum

[Kilroy, a young American Everyone, arrives on the Camino Real, a mystical street where the rich and powerful have all the privileges (they live in the luxurious Siete Mares Hotel on one side of the stage and the poor starve and die on Skid Row, on the other side of the stage). Kilroy discovers that not even the poorest of the poor will befriend him — they can't afford to.]

KILROY: (*Genially, to all present.*) Ha ha! (*Then he walks up to the Officer by the terrace of the Siete Mares.*) Buenas dias, señor. (*He gets no response — barely even a glance.*) Habla Inglesia? Usted?

OFFICER: What is it that you want?

KILROY: Where is Western Union or Wells-Fargo? I got to send a wire to some friends in the States.

OFFICER: No hay Western Union, no hay Wells-Fargo.

KILROY: That is very peculiar. I never struck a town yet that didn't have one or the other. I just got off a boat. Lousiest frigging tub I ever shipped on, one continual hell it was, all the way up from Rio. And me sick, too. I picked up one of those tropical fevers. No sick-bay on the tub, no doctor, no medicine or nothing, not even one quinine pill, and I was burning up with Christ knows how much fever. I couldn't make them understand I was sick. I got a bad heart, too. I had to retire from the prize ring because of my heart. I was the light heavyweight champion of the West Coast, won those gloves! — before my ticker went bad. — Feel my chest! Go on, feel it! Feel it. I've got a heart in my chest as big as the head of a baby. Ha ha! They stood me in front of a screen that makes you transparent and that's what they seen inside me, a heart in my chest as big as the head of a baby! With something like that you don't need the Gypsy to tell you, "Time is short, Baby — get ready to hitch on wings!" The medics wouldn't OK me for no more fights. They said to give up liquor and smoking and sex! — To give up sex! I used to believe a man couldn't live without sex — but he can — if he wants to! My real true woman, my wife, she would have stuck with me, but it was all spoiled with her being scared and me, too, that a real hard kiss would kill me! — So one night while she was sleeping I wrote her good-bye . . . (*He notices the lack of attention in the Officer: he grins.*) No comprendo the lingo?

OFFICER: What is it you want?

KILROY: Excuse my ignorance, but what place is this? What is this country and what is the name of this town? I know it seems funny of me to ask such a question. Loco! But I was so glad to get off that rotten tub that I didn't ask nothing of no one except my pay — and I got short-changed on that. I have trouble counting these pesos or Whatzit-you-call-'em. (*He jerks out his wallet.*) All-a-this-here. In the States that pile of lettuce would make you a plutocrat! — But I bet you this stuff don't add up to fifty dollars American coin. Ha ha!

OFFICER: Ha ha.

KILROY: Ha ha!

OFFICER: (*Making it sound like a death-rattle.*) Ha-ha-ha-ha-ha. (*He turns and starts into the cantina. Kilroy grabs his arm.*)

KILROY: Hey!

OFFICER: What is it you want?

KILROY: What is the name of this country and this town? (*The Officer thrusts his elbow in Kilroy's stomach and twists his arm loose with a Spanish curse. He kicks the swinging doors open and enters the cantina.*) Brass hats are the same everywhere.

(*As soon as the Officer goes, the Street People come forward and crowd about Kilroy with their wheedling cries.*)

STREET PEOPLE: Dulces, dulces! Lotería! Lotería! Pasteles, café con leche!

KILROY: No caree, no caree!

(*The prostitute creeps up to him and grins.*)

ROSITA: Love? Love?

KILROY: What did you say?

ROSITA: *Love?*

KILROY: Sorry — I don't feature that. (*To audience.*) I have ideals.

(*The Gypsy appears on the roof of her establishment with Esmeralda whom she secures with handcuffs to the iron railing.*)

GYPSY: Stay there while I give the pitch! (*She then advances with a portable microphone.*) Testing! One, two, three, four!

NURSIE: (*From offstage.*) You're on the air!

GYPSY'S LOUDSPEAKER: Are you perplexed by something? Are you tired out and confused? Do you have a fever? (*Kilroy looks around for the source of the voice.*) Do you feel yourself to be spiritually unprepared for the age of exploding atoms? Do you distrust newspapers? Are you suspicious of governments? Have you arrived at a point on the Camino Real where the walls converge not in the distance but right in front of your nose? Does further progress appear impossi-

ble to you? Are you afraid of anything at all? Afraid of your heart-
beat? Or the eyes of strangers! Afraid of not breathing? Do you wish
that things could be straight and simple again as they were in your
childhood? Would you like to go back to Kindy Garten?

*(Rosita has crept up to Kilroy as he listens. She reaches out to him. At the
same time a Pickpocket lifts his wallet.)*

KILROY: *(Catching the whore's wrist.)* Keep y'r hands off me, y' dirty ole
bag! No caree putas! No loteria, no dulces, nada — so get away! Va-
moose! All of you! Quick picking at me! *(He reaches in his pocket and
jerks out a handful of small copper and silver coins which he flings disgust-
edly down the street. The grotesque people scramble after it with their in-
human cries. Kilroy goes on a few steps — then stops short — feeling the
back pocket of his dungarees. Then he lets out a startled cry.)* Robbed!
My God, I've been robbed! *(The street people scatter to the walls.)*
Which of you got my wallet? *Which* of you dirty — ? Shh — Uh!
*(They mumble with gestures of incomprehension. He marches back to the
entrance to the hotel.)* Hey! Officer! Official! — General! *(The Officer
finally lounges out of the hotel entrance and glances at Kilroy.)* Tiende?
One of them's got my wallet! Picked it out of my pocket with that
old whore there was groping me! Don't you comprendo?

OFFICER: Nobody rob you. You don't have no pesos.

KILROY: Huh?

OFFICER: You just dreaming that you have money. You don't ever have
money. Nunca. Nada! *(He spits between his teeth.)* Loco… *(The officer crosses to the fountain. Kilroy stares at him, then bawls out.)*

KILROY: *(To the Street People.)* We'll see what the American Embassy
has to say about this! I'll go to the American Consul. Whichever of
you rotten spivs lifted my wallet is going to jail — calaboose! I hope
I have made myself plain. If not, I will make myself plainer! *(There
are scattered laughs among the crowd. He crosses to the fountain. He notices the body of the no longer Survivor, kneels beside it, shakes it, turns it
over, springs up and shouts.)* Hey! This guy is dead! *(There is the sound*

of the Streetcleaners' piping. *They trundle their white barrel into the plaza from one of the downstage arches. The appearance of these men undergoes a progressive alteration through the play. When they first appear they are almost like any such public servants in a tropical country; their white jackets are dirtier than the musicians' and some of the stains are red. They have on white caps with black visors. They are continually exchanging sly jokes and giggling unpleasantly together. Lord Mulligan has come out upon the terrace and as they pass him, they pause for a moment, point at him, snicker. He is extremely discomfited by this impertinence, touches his chest as if he felt a palpitation and turns back inside. Kilroy yells to the advancing Streetcleaners.*) There's a dead man layin' here! (*They giggle again. Briskly they lift the body and stuff it into the barrel; then trundle it off, looking back at Kilroy, giggling, whispering. They return under the downstage arch through which they entered. Kilroy, in a low, shocked voice.*) What *is* this place? What kind of hassle have I got myself into?

LOUDSPEAKER: If anyone on the Camino is bewildered, come to the Gypsy. A poco dinero will tickle the Gypsy's palm and give her visions!

ABDULLAH: (*Giving Kilroy a card.*) Man, whenever you see those three brass balls on a street, you don't have to look a long ways for a Gypsy. No le' me think. I am faced with three problems. One: I'm hungry. Two: I'm lonely. Three: I'm in a place where I don't know what it is or how I go there! First action that's indicated is to — cash in on something — Well . . . let's see . . .

(*Honky-tonk music fades in at this point and the Skid Row façade begins to light up for the evening. There is the Gypsy's stall with its cabalistic devices, its sectional cranium and palm, the luminous brass balls overhanging the entrance to the Loan Shark and his window filled with a vast assortment of hocked articles for sale: trumpets, banjos, fur coats, tuxedos, a gown of scarlet sequins, loops of pearls and rhinestones. Dimly behind this display is a neon sign in three pastel colors, pink, green, and blue. It fades softly in and out and it says: "Magic Tricks Jokes." There is also the advertisement of a flea-bag hotel or flophouse called "Ritz Men Only."*)

This sign is also pale neon or luminous paint, and only the entrance is on the street floor, the rooms are above the Loan Shark and Gypsy's stall. One of the windows of this upper story is practical. Figures appear in it sometimes, leaning out as if suffocating or to hawk and spit into the street below. This side of the street should have all the color and animation that are permitted by the resources of the production. There may be moments of dance-like action [a fight, a seduction, sale of narcotics, arrest, etc.].)

KILROY: (*To the audience from the apron.*) What've I got to cash in on? My golden gloves? Never! I'll say that once more, never! The silver-framed photo of my One True Woman? Never! Repeat that! Never! What else have I got of a detachable and negotiable nature? Oh! My ruby-and-emerald belt with the word CHAMP on it. (*He whips it off his pants.*) This is not necessary to hold on my pants, but this is a precious reminder of the sweet used-to-be. Oh, well. Sometimes a man has got to hock his sweet used-to-be in order to finance his present situation . . . (*He enters the Loan Shark's. A Drunken Bum leans out the practical window of the "Ritz Men Only" and shouts.*)

BUM: O Jack o' Diamonds, you robbed my pockets, you robbed my pockets of silver and gold. (*He jerks the window shade down.*)

****

from **CAT ON A HOT TIN ROOF** (1955)
from Act One, Scene One

CHARACTERS

Brick
Margaret
Mae
Sonny
Gooper

[The family of Big Daddy Pollitt, a plantation owner in the Mississippi
Delta, is celebrating his birthday — although some in the family know
that he is dying of cancer, and have kept the fact from him and from
his wife, Big Mama. His son Gooper, daughter-in-law Mae, and their
five children have arrived — to celebrate but also to break the bad
news to Big Mama and to make certain that the bulk of Big Daddy's
vast wealth passes to them. Big Daddy's younger son, Brick, broke his
ankle the night before while drunkenly trying to run hurdles on the
high school track. He and his wife, Maggie, have slept separately, and
Brick has begun to drink heavily, since the death of his best friend,
Skipper. In this scene, Maggie tries to help Brick pull himself together
for the birthday party going on downstairs.]

BRICK: Will you do me a favor?
MARGARET: Maybe I will. What favor?
BRICK: Just keep your voice down!
MARGARET: (_In a hoarse whisper._) I'll do you a favor, I'll speak in a whis-
    per, if not shut up completely, if _you_ will do me a favor and make that
    drink your last one till after the party.
BRICK: What party?
MARGARET: Big Daddy's birthday party.
BRICK: Is this Big Daddy's birthday?

MARGARET: You know this is Big Daddy's birthday!

BRICK: No, I don't, I forgot it.

MARGARET: Well, I remembered it for you . . .

(They are both speaking as breathlessly as a pair of kids after a fight, drawing deep exhausted breaths and looking at each other with faraway eyes, shaking and panting together as if they had broken apart from a violent struggle.)

BRICK: Good for you, Maggie.

MARGARET: You just have to scribble a few lines on this card.

BRICK: You scribble something, Maggie.

MARGARET: It's got to be your handwriting; it's your present, I've given him my present; it's got to be your handwriting!

(The tension between them is building again, the voices becoming shrill once more.)

BRICK: I didn't get him a present.

MARGARET: I got one for you.

BRICK: All right. You write the card, then.

MARGARET: And have him know you didn't remember his birthday?

BRICK: I didn't remember his birthday.

MARGARET: You don't have to prove you didn't!

BRICK: I don't want to fool him about it.

MARGARET: Just write "Love, Brick!" for God's —

BRICK: No.

MARGARET: You've *got* to!

BRICK: I don't have to do anything I don't want to do. You keep forgetting the conditions on which I agreed to stay on living with you.

MARGARET: *(Out before she knows it.)* I'm not living with you. We occupy the same cage.

BRICK: You've got to remember the conditions agreed on.

SONNY: *(Offstage.)* Mommy, give it to me. I had it first.

MAE: Hush.

MARGARET: They're impossible conditions!

BRICK: Then why don't you — ?

SONNY: I want it, I want it!

MAE: Get away!

MARGARET: HUSH! Who is out there? Is somebody at the door?

(There are footsteps in the hall.)

MAE: (*Outside.*) May I enter a moment?

MARGARET: Oh, *you!* Sure. Come in, Mae.

(Mae enters bearing aloft the bow of a young lady's archery set.)

MAE: Brick, is this thing yours?

MARGARET: Why, Sister Woman — that's my Diana Trophy. Won it at the intercollegiate contest on the Ole Miss campus.

MAE: It's a mighty dangerous thing to leave exposed round a house full of nawmal rid-blooded children attracted t'weapons.

MARGARET: "Nawmal rid-blooded children attracted t'weapons" ought t'be taught to keep their hands off things that don't belong to them.

MAE: Maggie, honey, if you had children of your own you'd know how funny that is. Will you please lock this up and put the key out of reach?

MARGARET: Sister Woman, nobody is plotting the destruction of your kiddies. — Brick and I still have our special archers' license. We're goin deer-huntin' on Moon Lake as soon as the season starts. I love to run with dogs through chilly woods, run, run, leap over obstructions — (*She goes into the closet carrying the bow.*)

MAE: How's the injured ankle, Brick?

BRICK: Doesn't hurt. Just itches.

MAE: Oh, my! Brick — Brick, you should've been downstairs after supper! Kiddies put on a show. Polly played the piano, Buster and Sonny drums, an' then they turned out the lights an' Dixie and Trixie puhfawmed a toe dance in fairy costume with *spahkluhs!* Big Daddy just beamed! He just beamed!

MARGARET: (*From the closet with a sharp laugh.*) Oh, I bet. It breaks my heart that we missed it! (*She reenters.*) But Mae? Why did y'give dawgs' names to all your kiddies?

MAE: *Dogs'* names?

MARGARET: (*Sweetly.*) Dixie, Trixie, Buster, Sonny, Polly!— Sounds like four dogs and a parrot . . .

MAE: Maggie? (*Margaret turns with a smile.*) Why are you so catty?

MARGARET: Cause I'm a cat! But why can't *you* take a joke, Sister Woman?

MAE: Nothin' please me more than a joke that's funny. You know the real names of our kiddies. Buster's real name is Robert. Sonny's real name is Saunders. Trixie's real name is Marlene and Dixie's — (*Gooper downstairs calls for her. "Hey, Mae Sister Woman, intermission is over!" — She rushes to the door, saying.*) Intermission is over! See ya later!

MARGARET: I wonder what Dixie's real name is?

BRICK: Maggie, being catty doesn't help things any . . .

MARGARET: I know! WHY! — Am I so catty? — Cause I'm consumed with envy an' eaten up with longing? — Brick, I'm going to lay out your beautiful Shantung silk suit from Rome and one of your monogrammed silk shirts. I'll put your cuff links in it, those lovely sapphires I get you to wear so rarely . . .

BRICK: I can't get trousers on over this plaster cast.

MARGARET: Yes, you can, I'll help you.

BRICK: I'm not going to get dressed, Maggie.

MARGARET: Will you just put on a pair of white silk pajamas?

BRICK: Yes, I'll do that, Maggie.

MARGARET: *Thank* you, thank you so *much!*

BRICK: Don't mention it.

MARGARET: *Oh, Brick!* How long does it have t'go on? This punishment? Haven't I done time enough, haven't I served my term, can't I apply for a — pardon?

BRICK: Maggie, you're spoiling my liquor. Lately your voice always sounds like you'd been running upstairs to warn somebody that the house was on fire!

MARGARET: Well, no wonder, no wonder. Y'know what I feel like, Brick? *I feel all the time like a cat on a hot tin roof!*

BRICK: Then jump off the roof, jump off it, cats can jump off roofs and land on their four feet uninjured!

MARGARET: Oh, yes!

BRICK: Do it! — fo' God's sake, do it...

MARGARET: Do what?

BRICK: Take a lover!

MARGARET: I can't see a man but you! Even with my eyes closed, I just see you! Why don't you get ugly, Brick, why don't you please get fat or ugly or something so I could stand it? (*She rushes to the hall door, opens it, listens.*) The concert is still going on! Bravo, no-necks, bravo! (*She slams and locks door fiercely.*)

BRICK: What did you lock the door for?

MARGARET: To give us a little privacy for a while.

BRICK: You know better, Maggie.

MARGARET: No, I don't know better . . . (*She rushes to galley doors, draws the rose-silk drapes across them.*)

BRICK: Don't make a fool of yourself.

MARGARET: I don't mind makin' a fool of myself over you!

BRICK: I mind, Maggie. I feel embarrassed for you.

MARGARET: Feel embarrassed! But don't continue my torture. I can't love on and on under these circumstances.

BRICK: You agreed to —

MARGARET: I know but —

BRICK: — Accept that condition!

MARGARET: I CAN'T! CAN'T! CAN'T! (*She seizes his shoulder.*)

****

from **VIEUX CARRÉ** (1977)

Scene Twelve

CHARACTERS

    Writer
    Mrs. Wire
    Nursie
    Jane
    Tye

[The writer, a young man with literary aspirations, has moved to a ramshackle boardinghouse in the French Quarter of New Orleans in 1938. He meets the various residents of the boardinghouse, which include Jane, a young fashion illustrator, and her boyfriend, Tye, a barker at a French Quarter strip club; Nightingale, an artist; and two old, starving aristocrats fallen on hard times, Miss Carrie and Mary Maude. The landlord is the formidable Mrs. Wire, ever on the lookout for tenants trying to skip out on their rent or bringing home partners for sex. Many years previously, she lost her son to her ex-husband in a custody battle, and lately has been mistaking the writer for him. In this, the play's last scene, the writer is about to leave the boarding house for the wide world outside.]

WRITER: (*As narrator.*) She was watching him with an unspoken question in her eyes, a little resentful now.

MRS. WIRE'S VOICE: (*From offstage, curiously altered.*) Why are those stairs so dark?

(*The light in the studio area is dimmed to half during the brief scene that follows. The writer rises and stands apprehensively alert as Mrs. Wire becomes visible in a yellowed silk robe with torn lace, a reliquary garment. Her hair is loose, her steps unsteady, her eyes hallucinated.)*

WRITER: (*Crossing from the studio, dismayed.*) Is that you, Mrs. Wire?

MRS. WIRE: Now, Timmy, Timmy, you mustn't cry every time Daddy gets home from the road and naturally wants to be in bed just with Mommy. It's Daddy's privilege, Mommy's — obligation. You'll understand when you're older — You see, Daddy finds Mommy attractive.

WRITER: (*Backing away from the cubicle entrance.*) Mrs. Wire, you're dreaming.

MRS. WIRE: Things between grownups in love and marriage can't be told to a child. (*She sits on the writer's cot.*) Now lie down and Mommy will sing you a little sleepy-time song. (*She is staring into space. He moves to the cubicle entrance, the candle is turned over and snuffed out.*)

MRS. WIRE: Rock-a-by, baby, in a tree top, if the wind blows, the cradle will rock . . .

WRITER: Mrs. Wire, I'm not Timothy, I'm not Tim, I'm not Timmy. (*He touches her.*)

MRS. WIRE: Dear child given to me of love . . .

WRITER: Mrs. Wire, I'm not your child. I am nobody's child. Was maybe, but not now. I've grown into a man, about to take his first step out of this waiting station into the world.

MRS. WIRE: Mummy knows you're scared sleeping alone in the dark. But the Lord gave us dark for sleep and Daddy don't like to find you took his rightful place . . .

WRITER: Mrs. Wire, I'm no relation to you, none but a tenant that earned his keep a while . . . Nursie! Nursie!

NURSIE: (*Approaching.*) She gone up there? (*Nursie appears.*) She gets these spells, goes back in time. I think it musta been all that Azalea Festival excitement done it.

MRS. WIRE: If the bough breaks, the cradle will fall . . .

NURSIE: (*At the cubicle entrance.*) Mizz Wire, it's Nursie. I'll take you back downstairs.

MRS. WIRE: (*Rousing a bit.*) It all seems so real. — I even remember lovemaking.

NURSIE: Get up, Mizz Wire, come down with Nursie

MRS. WIRE: (*Accepting Nursie's support.*) Now I'm — old. (*They withdraw from the light.*)

MRS. WIRE'S VOICE: Ahhhhhhhh . . . Ahhhhhhhh . . . Ahhhh . . . Ahhhhh . . . (*This expression of despair is lost in the murmur of the winds. The writer sinks onto his cot; the angel of the alcove appears in the dusk.*)

WRITER: Grand! (*She lifts her hand in a valedictory gesture.*) I guess angels warn you to leave a place by leaving before you. (*The light dims in the cubicle as the writer begins to pack and builds back up in the studio. The writer returns to the edge of the studio light.*)

JANE: You said you were going to get dressed and go back to your place of employment and resume the pitch for the ladies.

TYE: What did you say, babe? (*He has finished dressing and is now at the mirror, absorbed in combing his hair. Jane utters a soft, involuntary laugh.*)

JANE: A hundred dollars, the price and worth it, certainly worth it. I must be much in your debt, way over my means to pay off!

TYE: Well, I ain't paid to make a bad appearance at work. (*He puts on a sport shirt with girls in grass skirts printed on it.*)

JANE: I hate that shirt.

TYE: I know you think it's tacky. Well, I'm tacky, and it's the only clean one I got.

JANE: It isn't clean, not really. And does it express much grief over the Champagne Girls violent departure to Spain?

TYE: Do you have to hit me with that? What reason . . . ?

JANE: I've really got no reason to hit a goddamn soul but myself that lacked pride to keep my secrets. You know I shouldn't have told you about my — intentions, I should have just slipped away. The

Brazilian was far from attractive but — my circumstances required some drastic — compromises.

TYE: (*Crouching beside her.*) You're talking no sense, Jane. The Brazilian's out of the picture; those steps on the stairs were steps of hospital workers coming to take a — pick a dying fruit outa the place.

JANE: *Do you think I expect you back here again?* You'll say yes, assure me now as if forever — but — reconsider — the moment of impulse . . .

TYE: Cut some slack for me Babe. We all gotta cut some slack for each other in this fucking world. Lissen. You don't have to sweat it.

JANE: Give me another remission; one that lasts!

TYE: Gotta go now, it's late, after dark, and I'm dressed.

JANE: Well, zip your fly up unless you're now in the show.

(She rises and zips up his fly, touches his face and throat with trembling fingers.)

TYE: Jane, we got love between us! Don't you know that?

JANE: (*Not harshly.*) Lovely old word, love, it's traveled a long way, Tye.

TYE: And still's a long way to go. Hate to leave you alone, but —

JANE: I'm not alone. I've got Beret. An animal is a comforting presence sometimes. I wonder if they'd admit her to St. Vincents?

TYE: St. Vincents?

JANE: That charity hospital where they took the painter called Nightingale.

TYE: You ain't going there, honey.

JANE: It strikes me as being a likely destination.

TYE: Why?

JANE: I watched you dress. I didn't exist for you. Nothing existed for you but your image in the mirror. Understandably so. (*With her last strength she draws herself up.*)

TYE: What's understandable, Jane? — You got a fever? (*He rises, too, and stretches out a hand to touch her forehead. She knocks it away.*)

JANE: What's understandable is your present convenience is about to become an incumberence. An invalid, of no use, financial or sexual.

Sickness is repellant, Tye, demands more care and gives less and less in return. The person you loved — assuming you *did* love when she was still useful — is now, is now as absorbed in preparing herself for oblivion as you were absorbed in your — your image in the — mirror!

TYE: (*Frightened by her vehemence.*) Hey, Jane! (*Again she strikes away his extended hand.*)

JANE: Readies herself for it as you do for the street! (*She continues as to herself.*) — Withdraws into another dimension. Is indifferent to you except as caretaker — ! Is less aware of you than of — (*Panting, she looks up slowly through the skylight.*) — Sky that's visible to her from her bed under the skylight — At night, these — filmy white clouds, they move, they drift over the roofs of the Vieux Carré so close that if you have fever you feel as if you could touch them, and bits would come off on your fingers, soft as — cotton candy —

TYE: Rest, Babe. I'll be back early. I'll get Smokey to take over for me at midnight, and I'll come back with tamales and a bottle of vino. (*He crosses out of the light. She rushes to the door.*)

JANE: *No, no, not before daybreak and with a new needle mark on your arm.* Beret? Beret! (*She staggers wildly out of the light, calling the cat again and again.*)

WRITER: I lifted her from the floor where she'd fallen . . . (*Various voices are heard exclaiming around the house.*) (*The writer reappears in the studio area supporting Jane, who appears half conscious.*) Jane? Jane?

JANE: — My cat, I scared it away…

NURSIE: (*Offstage.*) What is goin' on up there?

WRITER: She was frightened by something.

JANE: I lost my cat, that's all. — They don't understand . . . (*The writer places her on the bed.*) Alone. I'm alone.

WRITER: She'll be back. Jane didn't seem to hear me. She was looking up at the skylight.

JANE: It isn't blue anymore, it suddenly turned quite dark.

WRITER: It was dark as the question in her eyes.

(The blues piano fades in.)

JANE: It's black as the piano man playing around the corner.

WRITER: It must be after six. What's the time now?

JANE: Time? What? Oh. Time. My sight is blurred. *(She shows him her wristwatch.)* Can't make out that luminous dial, can you?

WRITER: It says five of twelve.

JANE: An improbable hour. Must have run down.

WRITER: I'll take it off. To wind it. *(He puts the watch to his ear.)* I'm afraid it's broken.

JANE: *(Vaguely.)* I hadn't noticed — lately — I tell time by the sky.

WRITER: His name was Sky.

JANE: Tye . . . .

WRITER: No, not Tye. Sky was the name of someone who offered me a ride West.

JANE: — I've had fever all day. Did you come to ask me a question?

WRITER: I said I planned a trip to the West Coast with this young vagrant, a musician.

JANE: Young vagrants are irresponsible. I'm not at all surprised — He let you down? Well. I have travel plans, too.

WRITER: With Tye?

JANE: No, I was going alone, not with Tye. What are you doing there?

WRITER: Setting up the chessboard. Want to play?

JANE: Oh, Yes, you said you play. I'd have a partner for once. But my concentration's — I warn you — it's likely to be — impaired.

WRITER: Want to play white or black?

JANE: You choose. *(The piano fades in. Jane looks about in a confused way.)*

WRITER: Black. In honor of the musician around the corner.

JANE: — He's playing something appropriate to the occasion as if I'd phoned in a request. How's it go? So familiar.

WRITER: "Makes no difference how things break, I'll still get by somehow. I'm not sorry, cause it makes no difference now."

JANE: Each of us abandoned to the other. You know this is almost our first private conversation. *(She nearly falls to the floor. He catches here*

78

and supports her to the chair at the upstage side of the table.) Shall we play, let's do. With no distraction at all. (*She seems unable to move; she has a frozen attitude.*) (*There is a distant sustained high note from Sky's clarinet. They both hear it. Jane tries to distract the writer's attention from the sound and continues quickly with feverish animation. The sound of the clarinet becomes more urgent.*) Vagrants, I can tell you about them. From experience. Incorrigibly delinquent. Purposeless. Addictive. Grab at you for support when support's what *you* need — gone? Whistling down the last flight, such a lively popular tune. Well, I have travel plans, but in the company of no charming young vagrant. Love Mediterranean countries but somehow missed Spain. I plan to go. Now! Madrid, to visit the Prado, most celebrated museum of all. Admire the Goyas, El Grecos. Hire a car to cross the — gold plains of Toledo.

WRITER: Jane, you don't have to make up stories, I hear your talk with Tye — all of it.

JANE: Then you must have heard his leaving. How his steps picked up speed on the second flight down — started whistling . . .

WRITER: He always whistles down stairs — it's habitual to him — you mustn't attach special meaning to it.

(*The clarinet music is closer. The sound penetrates the shut windows.*)

JANE: At night the Quarter's so full of jazz music, so many entertainers. Isn't it now your move?

WRITER: (*Embarrassed.*) It's your move, Jane.

JANE: (*Relinquishing her game.*) No yours — Your vagrant musician is late but you're not forgotten.

WRITER: A call down, ask him to wait till midnight when Tye said he'll be back.

JANE: With tamales and vino to celebrate — (*She staggers to the window, shatters a pane of glass and shouts.*) — Your friend's coming right down, just picking up his luggage! (*She leans against the wall, panting, her bleeding hand behind her*.) Now go, quick. He might not wait, you'd regret it.

WRITER: Can't I do something for you?

JANE: Pour me three fingers of bourbon. (*She has returned to the table. He pours the shot.*) Now hurry, hurry. I know that Tye will be back early tonight.

WRITER: Yes, of course he will . . .

(He crosses from the studio light)

JANE: (*Smiling somewhat bitterly.*) Naturally, yes, how could I possibly doubt it. With tamales and vino . . . (*She uncloses her fist; the blood is running from palm to wrist. The writer picks up a cardboard laundry box and the typewriter case.*)

WRITER: As I left, I glanced at Jane's door. She seemed to be or was pretending to be — absorbed in her solitary chess game. I went down the second flight and on the cot in the dark passageway was — (*He calls out.*) Beret? (*For the first time the cat is visible, white and fluffy as a piece of cloud. Nursie looms dimly behind him, her dark solemn face lamplit.*)

NURSIE: It's the cat Miss Sparks come runnin' after.

WRITER: Take it to her, Nursie. She's alone up there.

MRS. WIRE: Now watch out, boy. Be careful of the future. It's a long ways for the young. Some makes it and other git lost.

WRITER: I know . . . (*He turns to the audience.*) I stood by the door uncertainly for a moment or two. I must have been frightened of it . . .

MRS. WIRE: Can you see the door?

WRITER: Yes — but to open it is a desperate undertaking . . . ! (*He does, hesitantly. Transparencies close from either wing. Dim spots of light touch each character of the play in a characteristic position. As he first draws the door open, he is forced back a few steps by a cacophony of sound: the waiting storm of his future — mechanical wracking cries of pain and pleasure, snatches of song. It fades out. Again there is the urgent call of the clarinet.*

He crosses to the open door.) They're disappearing behind me. Going. People you've known in places do that: they go when you go. The Earth seems to swallow them up. The walls absorb them like moisture, remain with you only as ghosts; their voices are echoes, fading but remembered. (*The clarinet calls again. Turns for a moment at the door.*) This house is empty now.

****

THE READING ROOM

YOUNG ACTORS AND THEIR TEACHERS

Boxill, Roger. *Tennessee Williams*. London: Macmillan, 1987.

Hirsch, Foster. *A Portrait of the Artist: The Plays of Tennessee Williams*. Port Washington, N.Y.: Kennikat, 1979.

Leavitt, Richard. *The World of Tennessee Williams*. New York: Putnam, 1978.

Spoto, Donald. *The Kindness of Strangers: The Life of Tennessee Williams*. New York: Ballantine: 1986.

SCHOLARS, STUDENTS, PROFESSORS

Adams, Julie. *Versions of Heroism in Modern American Drama: Redefinitions by Miller, Williams, O'Neill and Anderson*. London: Macmillan, 1991.

Adler, Thomas P. *"A Streetcar Named Desire": The Moth and the Lantern*. Boston: Twayne, 1990.

_____. *American Drama 1940–1960: A Critical History*. New York: Twayne, 1994.

Bigsby, C. W. E. *Modern American Drama 1945–1990*. Cambridge: Cambridge University Press, 1992.

Choukri, Mohamed. *Tennessee Williams in Tangier*. Trans. Paul Bowles. Santa Barbara, Calif.: Cadmus, 1979.

Clurman, Harold. *The Divine Pastime*. New York: Macmillan, 1984.

Debusscher, Gilbert. "Creative Rewriting: European and American Influences on the Drama of Tennessee Williams." *Cambridge Companion to Tennessee Williams*. Ed. Matthew C. Roudane. Cambridge: Cambridge University Press, 1997. 167–188.

Falk, Signi L. *Tennessee Williams*. Boston: Twayne, 1978.

This extensive bibliography lists books about the playwright according to whom the books might be of interest. If you would like to research further something that interests you in the text, lists of references, sources cited, and editions used in this book are found in this section.

Fedder, Norman J. *The Influence of D. H. Lawrence on Tennessee Williams.* The Hague: Mouton, 1966.

Gross, Robert, ed. *Tennessee Williams: A Casebook.* New York: Routledge, 2001.

Hale, Allean, "The Secret Script of Tennessee Williams." *The Southern Review* 27 (April 1991): 363–375.

Holditch, Kenneth. "The Last Frontier of Bohemia: Tennessee Williams in New Orleans." *Southern Quarterly* 23 no. 2 (1985): 12.

Kaplan, David. *Tennessee Williams in Provincetown.* East Brunswick, N.J.: Hanson, 2006.

Kolin, Philip C., ed. *Confronting Tennessee Williams's "A Streetcar Named Desire": Essays in Critical Pluralism.* Westport, Conn.: Greenwood Press, 1993.

Londré, Felicia Hardison. *Tennessee Williams.* New York: Ungar, 1979.

Murphy, Brenda. *Tennessee Williams and Elia Kazan.* Cambridge: Cambridge University Press, 1992.

Parker, R. B., ed. *The Glass Menagerie: A Collection of Critical Essays.* Englewood Cliffs, N.J.: Prentice-Hall, 1983.

Phillips, Gene D. *The Films of Tennessee Williams.* East Brunswick, N.J.: Associated University Presses, 1980.

Savran, David. *Communists, Cowboys and Queers: The Politics of Masculinity in the Works of Arthur Miller and Tennessee Williams.* Minneapolis: University of Minnesota Press, 1992.

Smith-Howard, Myeia, and Greta Heintzelman. *Critical Companion to Tennessee Williams.* New York: Checkmark Books, 2005.

Stanton, Stephen S., ed. *Tennessee Williams: A Collection of Critical Essays.* Englewood Cliffs, N.J.: Prentice-Hall, 1977.

Steen, Mike. *A Look at Tennessee Williams.* New York: Hawthorn, 1969.

Tharp, Jac, ed. *Tennessee Williams: A Tribute.* Jackson: University of Mississippi Press, 1977.

_____. *Tennessee Williams: Thirteen Essays.* Jackson: University of Mississippi Press, 1980.

Thompson, Judith J. *Tennessee Williams's Plays: Memory, Myth, and Symbol.* New York: Peter Lang, 1987.

Tischler, Nancy M. *Tennessee Williams: Rebellious Puritan.* New York: Citadel Press, 1961.

Voss, Ralph, ed. *Magical Muse: Millennial Essays on Tennessee Williams.* Tuscaloosa: University of Alabama Press, 2002.

Windham, Donald. *Lost Friendships: A Memoir of Truman Capote, Tennessee Williams and Others*. St. Paul, Minn.: Paragon House, 1989.

_____, ed. *Tennessee Williams's Letters to Donald Windham 1940–1965*. Athens, Ga.: University of Georgia Press, 1996.

THEATER, PRODUCERS

Crandall, George. *Tennessee Williams: A Descriptive Bibliography*. Pittsburgh: University of Pittsburgh Press, 1995.

Griffin, Alice. *Understanding Tennessee Williams*. Columbia: University of South Carolina, Press, 1995.

Miller, Jordan Y., ed. *Twentieth Century Interpretations of A Streetcar Named Desire: A Collection of Critical Essays*. Englewood Cliffs, N.J.: Prentice-Hall, 1971.

Paller, Michael. *Gentlemen Callers: Tennessee Williams, Homosexuality, and Mid-Twentieth-Century Drama*. New York: Palgrave Macmillan, 2005.

Williams, Dakin, and Shepherd Mead. *Tennessee Williams: An Intimate Biography*. Westminster, Md.: Arbor House, 1983.

Williams, Edwina, as told to Lucy Freeman. *Remember Me to Tom*. New York: Putnam, 1963.

ACTORS, DIRECTORS, THEATER PROFESSIONALS

Hale, Allean. "Early Williams: The Making of a Playwright." *The Cambridge Companion to Tennessee Williams*. Ed. Matthew Roudané. Cambridge: Cambridge University Press, 1997. 11–28.

Hayman, Ronald. *Tennessee Williams: Everyone Else Is an Audience*. New Haven, Conn.: Yale University Press, 1993.

Jackson, Esther Merle. *The Broken World of Tennessee Williams*. Madison: University of Wisconsin Press, 1965.

Kolin, Philip C. *Tennessee Williams: A Guide to Research and Performance*. Westport, Conn.: Greenwood Press, 1998.

Williams, Tennessee. *Camino Real*. 2nd ed. New York: New Directions, 1953. 25–33.

_____. *Cat on a Hot Tin Roof*. 5th ed. New York: New Directions, 1975. 33–41

_____. *The Glass Menagerie*. In *The Theatre of Tennessee Williams vol. 1*. 1971. New York: New Directions, 1990. 168–175, 276–285.

_____. *A Streetcar Named Desire.* In *The Theatre of Tennessee Williams vol. 1.* 1971. New York: New Directions, 1990. 168–175.

_____. *Orpheus Descending.* In *Tennessee Williams: The Plays 1957–1980.* 1st ed. New York: New Directions, 2000. 32–40.

_____. *Vieux Carré.* In *Tennessee Williams: The Plays 1957–1980.* 1st ed. New York: New Directions, 2000. 893–901

THE EDITIONS OF WILLIAMS' WORKS USED FOR THIS BOOK

Quoted excerpts from the plays are derived from *The Theatre of Tennessee Williams* vol. 108. New York: New Directions, 1971–1992 and *Fugitive Kind.* New York: New Directions, 2001.

SOURCES CITED IN THIS BOOK

Bloom, Harold, ed. *Modern Critical Views: Tennessee Williams.* New York: Chelsea House, 1987.

Clinton, Craig, "The Reprise of Tennessee Williams *Vieux Carré*: An Interview with Director Keith Hack." *Studies in American Drama, 1945–Present* 7 no. 2 (1992): 265–275.

Clurman, Harold. *The Fervent Years.* New York: Harcourt Brace Jovanovich, 1975.

Debusscher, Gilbert. "Minting Their Separate Wills: Tennessee Williams and Hart Crane." *Modern Critical Views: Tennessee Williams.* Ed. Harold Bloom. New York: Chelsea House, 1987. 113–130.

Debusscher, Gilbert. "Creative Rewriting: European and American Influences on the Drama of Tennessee Williams." *Cambridge Companion to Tennessee Williams.* Ed. Matthew C. Roudane. Cambridge: Cambridge University Press, 1997. 167–188.

Devlin, Albert J., ed. *Conversations with Tennessee Williams.* Jackson: University Press of Mississippi, 1986.

Devlin, Albert J., and Nancy M. Tischer, ed. *The Selected Letters of Tennessee Williams*, Vol 2 1945–1957. New York: New Directions, 2004.

_____. *Notebooks.* Ed. Margaret Bradham Thorson. New Haven: Yale University Press, 2006.

Evans, Oliver. *New Orleans.* New York: Macmillan, 1959.

Holditch, Kenneth, and Richard Freeman Leavitt. *Tennessee Williams and the South.* Jackson: University Press of Mississippi, 2002.

Kolin, Philip C., ed. *The Undiscovered Country: The Later Plays of Tennessee Williams*. New York: Peter Lang, 2002.

Leverich, Lyle. *Tom: The Unknown Tennessee Williams*. New York: Crown, 1995.

Oakley, Giles. *The Devil's Music: A History of the Blues*. New York: Taplinger, 1977.

Saddik, Annette. *The Politics of Reputation: The Critical Reception of Tennessee Williams' Later Plays*. London: Associated University Presses, 1999.

Williams, Tennessee. *The Selected Letters of Tennessee Williams*. Vol. 2 1945–1957. Ed. Devlin, Albert J. and Nancy M. Tischer, New York: New Directions, 2004.

_____. *Collected Stories*. New York: New Directions, 1985.

_____. *The Theatre of Tennessee Williams* Vol. 108. New York: New Directions, 1971–1992, and *Fugitive Kind*. New York: New Directions, 2001.

_____. "On a Streetcar Named Success." *The New York Times*. November 30, 1947.

_____. "Tennessee Williams Presents His POV." *New Selected Essays: Where I Live*. Ed. John S. Bak. New York: New Directions, 2009.

_____. "The Timeless World of the Play." *New Selected Essays: Where I Live*. Ed. John S. Bak. New York: New Directions, 2009.

Awards

"And the winner is . . . "

	PULITZER PRIZE	TONY AWARD	NY DRAMA CRITICS CIRCLE AWARD		
			Best American	Best Foreign	Best Play
1935	Zoe Akins *The Old Maid*	-	-		
1936	Robert E. Sherwood *Idiot's Delight*	-	Maxwell Anderson *Winterset*		
1937	Moss Hart and George S. Kaufman *You Can't Take It With You*	-	Maxwell Anderson *High Tor*		
1938	Thornton Wilder *Our Town*	-	John Steinbeck *Of Mice and Men*		
1939	Robert E. Sherwood *Abe Lincoln in Illinois*	-	No award		
1940	William Saroyan *The Time of Your Life*	-	William Saroyan *The Time of Your Life*		
1941	Robert E. Sherwood *There Shall Be No Night*	-	Lillian Hellman *Watch on the Rhine*		
1942	No Award	-	No Award		
1943	Thornton Wilder *The Skin of Our Teeth*	-	Sidney Kingsley *The Patriots*		
1944	No Award	-	No Award		
1945	Mary Chase *Harvey*	-	**Tennessee Williams** ***The Glass Managerie***		
1946	Russel Crouse and Howard Lindsay *State of the Union*	-	No Award		
1947	No Award	Arthur Miller *All My Sons*	Arthur Miller *All My Sons*		
1948	**Tennessee Williams** ***A Streetcar Named Desire***	Joshua Logan and Thomas Heggen *Mister Roberts*	**Tennessee Williams** ***A Streetcar Named Desire***		
1949	Arthur Miller *Death of a Salesman*	Arthur Miller *Death of a Salesman*	Arthur Miller *Death of a Salesman*		

	PULITZER PRIZE	TONY AWARD	NY DRAMA CRITICS CIRCLE AWARD		
			Best American	Best Foreign	Best Play
1950	Richard Rodgers *South Pacific*	T. S. Eliot *The Cocktail Party*	Carson McCullers *A Member of the Wedding*		
1951	No Award	**Tennessee Williams** **The Rose Tattoo**	Sidney Kingsley *Darkness at Noon*		
1952	Joseph Kramm *The Shrike*	Jan de Hartog *The Fourposter*	John van Druten *I Am a Camera*		
1953	William Inge *Picnic*	Arthur Miller *The Crucible*	William Inge *Picnic*		
1954	John Patrick *The Teahouse of the August Moon*	John Patrick *The Teahouse of the August Moon*	John Patrick *The Teahouse of the August Moon*		
1955	**Tennessee Williams** **Cat on a Hot Tin Roof**	Joseph Hayes *The Desperate Hours*	**Tennessee Williams** **Cat on a Hot Tin Roof**		
1956	Albert Hackett and Frances Goodrich *The Diary of Anne Frank*	Albert Hackett and Frances Goodrich *The Diary of Anne Frank*	Albert Hackett and Frances Goodrich *The Diary of Anne Frank*		
1957	Eugene O'Neill *Long Day's Journey Into Night*	Eugene O'Neill *Long Day's Journey Into Night*	Eugene O'Neill *Long Day's Journey Into Night*		
1958	Ketti Frings *Look Homeward, Angel*	Dore Schary *Sunrise at Campobello*	Ketti Frings *Look Homeward, Angel*		
1959	Archibald Macleish *J.B.*	Archibald Macleish *J.B.*	Lorraine Hansberry *A Raisin in the Sun*		
1960	Jerry Bock, music Sheldon Harnick, lyrics Jerome Wiedman, book George Abbott, book *Fiorello!*	William Gibson *The Miracle Worker*	Lillian Hellman *Toys in the Attic*		
1961	Tad Mosel *All the Way Home*	Jean Anouilh *Beckett*	Tad Mosel *All the Way Home*		
1962	Frank Loesser and Abe Burrows *How to Succeed in Business Without Really Trying*	Robert Bolt *A Man for All Seasons*	**Tennessee Williams** **The Night of the Iguana**	Richard Bolt *A Man for All Seasons*	No Award

INDEX

The entries in the index include highlights from the main In an Hour essay portion of the book.

ABOUT THE AUTHOR

Michael Paller is the Dramaturge and Director of Humanities at the American Conservatory Theater in San Francisco, where he is also a member of the core faculty of the M.F.A. Acting program. He is the author of *Gentlemen Callers: Tennessee Williams, Homosexuality and Mid-Twentieth Century Drama* (Palgrave Macmillan). He has taught at Purchase College and Columbia University and was the Dramaturge for the Russian premiere of Williams' *Small Craft Warnings* (directed by Richard Corley) at Moscow's Sovremennic Theatre. He has written for many publications, including *The Village Voice*, *The Washington Post*, *Newsday*, *The Cleveland Plain Dealer*, *Mirabella*, and others. He has degrees from Syracuse University and Columbia University.

DEDICATION
To Steven

ACKNOWLEDGMENTS

Smith and Kraus would like to thank New Directions Publishing Corp., whose enlightened permissions policy reflects an understanding that copyright law is intended to both protect the rights of creators of intellectual property as well as to encourage its use for the public good.

Know the playwright,
love the play.

Open a new door to theater study, performance, and
audience satisfaction with these Playwrights In an Hour titles.

ANCIENT GREEK

Aeschylus   Aristophanes   Euripides   Sophocles

RENAISSANCE

William Shakespeare

MODERN

Anton Chekhov   Noël Coward   Lorraine Hansberry
Henrik Ibsen   Arthur Miller   Molière   Eugene O'Neill
Arthur Schnitzler   George Bernard Shaw   August Strindberg
Frank Wedekind   Oscar Wilde   Thornton Wilder
Tennessee Williams

CONTEMPORARY

Edward Albee   Alan Ayckbourn   Samuel Beckett
Theresa Rebeck   Sarah Ruhl   Sam Shepard   Tom Stoppard
August Wilson

To purchase or for more information
visit our web site inanhourbooks.com